Lee Kuan Yew
School of Public Policy

BUILDING A GLOBAL
POLICY SCHOOL IN ASIA

Lee Kuan Yew
School of Public Policy

BUILDING A GLOBAL
POLICY SCHOOL IN ASIA

Kishore Mahbubani
Stavros N. Yiannouka
Scott A. Fritzen
Astrid S. Tuminez
Kenneth Paul Tan

Published by

World Scientific Publishing Co. Pte. Ltd.

5 Toh Tuck Link, Singapore 596224

USA office: 27 Warren Street, Suite 401-402, Hackensack, NJ 07601

UK office: 57 Shelton Street, Covent Garden, London WC2H 9HE

Library of Congress Cataloging-in-Publication Data
Lee Kuan Yew School of Public Policy : building a global policy school in Asia / by Kishore
Mahbubani ... [et al.].
   p. cm.
  Includes bibliographical references.
  ISBN 978-9814417211
  1. Lee Kuan Yew School of Public Policy. 2. Policy sciences--Study and teaching (Higher)--
Singapore. 3. Political planning--Study and teaching (Higher)--Singapore.
  I. Mahbubani, Kishore.
  JF1525.P6L43 2013
  320.6095957--dc23

                            2012029247

British Library Cataloguing-in-Publication Data
A catalogue record for this book is available from the British Library.

In-house Editor: Juliet Lee Ley Chin

Printed in Singapore.

Contents

Preface

Our School will be eternally grateful that Mr. Lee Kuan Yew turned 80 on 16 September 2003. Until that day came, Mr. Lee had steadfastly refused to attach his name to any institution or piece of infrastructure. He said, famously, that he had been to many developing countries where leaders had attached their names everywhere. And when they died, their names were scrubbed out. Indeed, during his 80th birthday dinner, as Senior Minister, Lee said, "We have studiously avoided the build-up of personality cults — displays of paintings, photos, statues of leaders. The only photos the government sponsors are those of the president and his wife."[1]

Eight years have passed since the Lee Kuan Yew School of Public Policy was formally launched on 4 August 2004. The Chinese believe that *8* is a lucky number. Since the number *80* has been a lucky number for our School, we thought that the 8th anniversary would provide a good opportunity to reflect on our successes, areas to improve on and future challenges.

We could have done this reflection in three possible forms. Firstly, we could have followed the preferred Singapore method of commissioning a coffee-table book, replete with wonderful photos telling a wonderful fairy tale of constant success. Secondly, we could have commissioned an eminent expert or a well-known writer to do an in-depth study and write a book on our experiences. That could have been expensive. We therefore chose a more cost-efficient yet hopefully authentic option

---

1   Speech by Senior Minister Lee Kuan Yew at his 80th birthday dinner organised by the People's Action Party at the Raffles Ballroom, Swissôtel The Stamford, 21 September 2003.

of asking a few key participants in the growth of the School to reflect on their experiences.

All five of us have been with the School for some years. Kishore and Scott were there from Day One, although Scott's experience is even a bit longer since he was involved in the preceding Public Policy Programme from 9 June 2000. Stavros has also been involved with the School almost from Day One, although he began his association originally in his McKinsey capacity. Kenneth joined us from the Political Science Department of the NUS on 1 March 2007 and Astrid did so on 1 September 2008. As Rashomon taught us, the same event can be seen and described from different perspectives. This compilation seeks to offer just that — our perspectives.

In writing this book, we are very cognizant of the fact that the success to date of the LKY School would not have been possible without the hard work and support of dozens of our colleagues, both faculty and administrative staff alike. This is therefore as much a story of their achievements as it is ours. We would also like to thank President Susilo Bambang Yudhoyono, Tony Blair, Helen Clark, Pascal Lamy, Lim Siong Guan, Joseph Nye, Tharman Shanmugaratnam, Montek Singh Ahluwalia, Anne-Marie Slaughter and Paul Volcker for their generous endorsements of this book.

As then Minister Mentor Lee Kuan Yew said on 3 November 2006, the mission of the School is to "improve governance in the countries in Asia by attracting promising students and administrators to compare governance in Asia, EU, and US and adopt the best models." We hope that we have gone some way towards fulfilling this mission.

Kishore Mahbubani
Stavros N. Yiannouka
Scott A. Fritzen
Astrid S. Tuminez
Kenneth Paul Tan
June 2012

About the Authors

 **Kishore Mahbubani** is Dean and Professor in the Practice of Public Policy at the Lee Kuan Yew School of Public Policy at the National University of Singapore. He previously served for 33 years in Singapore's diplomatic service and is recognised as an expert on Asian and world affairs. With the Singapore Foreign Service from 1971 to 2004, he had postings in Cambodia (where he served during the war in 1973–74), Malaysia, Washington DC and New York, where he served two stints as Singapore's Ambassador to the UN and as President of the UN Security Council in January 2001 and May 2002. He was Permanent Secretary at the Foreign Ministry from 1993 to 1998. Professor Mahbubani also serves in Boards and Councils of several institutions in Singapore, Europe and North America, including the Yale President's Council on International Activities (PCIA), Association of Professional Schools of International Affairs, Indian Prime Minister's Global Advisory Council, University of Bocconi International Advisory Committee, World Economic Forum — Global Agenda Council on China — and Chairman of the Lee Kuan Yew World City Prize Nominating Committee. In the world of ideas, Professor Mahbubani has spoken and published globally. His articles have appeared in a wide range of journals and newspapers, including *Foreign Affairs*, *Foreign Policy*, the *Washington Quarterly*, *Survival*, *American Interest*, the *National Interest*, *Time*, *Newsweek*, the *Financial Times* and *New York Times*. He has also been profiled in *The Economist* and in *Time Magazine*. He is the author of *Can Asians Think?* (published and

translated in Singapore, Canada, the US, Mexico, India, China Myanmar, Turkey and Malaysia), *Beyond The Age Of Innocence: Rebuilding Trust between America and the World* (published and translated in the US and China), and *The New Asian Hemisphere: the irresistible shift of global power to the East* (published and translated in the US, France, Germany, The Netherlands, Egypt, China, Korea, Japan, Indonesia, Italy, Taiwan and Vietnam). More information on his writings can be found at www.mahbubani.net.

Professor Mahbubani was awarded the President's Scholarship in 1967. He graduated with a first-class honours degree in Philosophy from the University of Singapore in 1971. From Dalhousie University, Canada, he received a Master's degree in Philosophy in 1976 and an honorary doctorate in 1995. He spent a year as a fellow at the Center for International Affairs at Harvard University from 1991 to 1992.

Professor Mahbubani was conferred The Public Administration Medal (Gold) by the Singapore Government in 1998. The Foreign Policy Association Medal was awarded to him in New York in June 2004 with the following opening citation: "A gifted diplomat, a student of history and philosophy, a provocative writer and an intuitive thinker". He was also listed as one of the top 100 public intellectuals in the world by *Foreign Policy* and *Prospect* magazines in September 2005, and included in the March 2009 *Financial Times'* list of Top 50 individuals (including Obama, Wen Jiabao and Sarkozy) who would shape the debate on the future of capitalism. Most recently, Professor Mahbubani was selected as one of *Foreign Policy's* Top Global Thinkers in 2010 and 2011. In 2011, he was described as "the muse of the Asian century".

Stavros N. Yiannouka was until 24 August 2012 the Executive Vice-Dean of the Lee Kuan Yew School of Public Policy at the National University of Singapore. He joined the LKY School in June 2005 to spearhead the implementation of the School's ambitious growth strategy, which he had helped develop as a management consultant with McKinsey & Company. Whilst at the LKY School,

Stavros built its successful, pan-Asian Executive Education business and led the School's branding, marketing and strategic partnership development efforts. Prior to joining the LKY School, he spent five years with McKinsey & Company from 2000 to 2005 serving private and public sector clients in Singapore, Indonesia, South Korea and Canada, predominantly in the financial services and healthcare industries. From 1995 to 1998, Stavros practised corporate law in the City of London with the firms Gouldens and Mayer, Brown & Platt. He holds an MBA (with Distinction) from the London Business School and an LLB (with Honours) from the University of Bristol, and is a member of the Law Society of England and Wales. A native of Cyprus, Stavros is married to Sherena Mistri, a Singaporean, and they have two children Stephania and Nicholas. On 25 August 2012, Stavros and his family will relocate to Doha, Qatar where he will join the Qatar Foundation as CEO of the World Innovation Summit for Education, a major initiative of the Foundation.

Scott A. Fritzen is currently serving as Associate Dean (Academic Affairs) of the Robert F. Wagner Graduate School of Public Service at New York University. He is on leave from the Lee Kuan Yew School of Public Policy at the National University of Singapore, where he served as Vice-Dean (Academic Affairs) from 2008 to 2011. He also served on the faculty of the LKY School and its predecessor Public Policy Programme of the Faculty of Arts and Social Sciences at the National University of Singapore since the year 2000.

Professor Fritzen specialises in the analysis of governance reform and capacity strengthening in developing and transition countries, with a particular interest in the comparative analysis of anti-corruption strategies, public sector decentralisation trends and the rise of global public policy education. He has taught many of the core management and administration courses in the school, as well as electives in public sector reform, negotiation and social policy.

Professor Fritzen's active consulting practice since 1994 in Asia has included over 35 assignments — most of which as team leader — for clients such as the World Bank, UNDP and Oxfam. He was the first American in the post-war era designated a Fulbright Fellow for Vietnam and has also lived for extended periods in Japan, Germany, Italy, Indonesia, and Zimbabwe. His Master in Public Affairs and Urban and Regional Planning degree and PhD in Public Affairs are both from the Woodrow Wilson School of Public and International Affairs, Princeton University.

When not in the classroom, Fritzen is usually only found on a rock climbing wall or cliff face, or playing with his children aged 5 and 7 (and occasionally both at the same time).

 **Astrid S. Tuminez** was Assistant Dean (Executive Education, 2008–2010) and Vice-Dean (Research, 2011–2012) of the Lee Kuan Yew School of Public Policy at the National University of Singapore. She came to the School with over two decades of experience in public policy analysis, philanthropy, research and project management, teaching and venture capital investment. Previously, she was Senior Research Associate of the Philippine Facilitation Project of the US Institute of Peace where, with US State Department funding, she assisted in peace negotiations between the Philippine government and the Moro Islamic Liberation Front.

Dr. Tuminez has been a Senior Advisor, Strategy and Programs, for the Salzburg Global Seminar. She is also the former Director of Research for alternative investments at AIG (American International Group) Global Investment Corp. In the early 1990s, she ran the Moscow office of the Harvard Project on Strengthening Democratic Institutions. From 1992 to 1998, she was a programme officer at the Carnegie Corporation of New York, responsible for grant-making in conflict prevention, the non-proliferation of weapons of mass destruction, and democratisation. She also worked with the Carnegie Commission on Preventing Deadly Conflict, chaired by former US Secretary of State Cyrus Vance and Dr. David Hamburg. She has been a consultant to The World Bank and an institutional sales/research professional at Brunswick Warburg, Inc. She holds a Master's from Harvard and a PhD from MIT.

Dr. Tuminez is a former Adjunct Fellow and a permanent member of the Council on Foreign Relations. Her publications include *Russian Nationalism Since 1856: Ideology and the Making of Foreign Policy* (Rowman and Littlefield, 2000), journal articles, essays, and opinion pieces for newspapers. Most recently, she published "Rising to the Top? A Report on Women's Leadership in Asia". She has been a US Institute of Peace Scholar, a Freeman Fellow of the Salzburg Seminar, a fellow at the Harvard Kennedy School, a Distinguished Alumna of Brigham Young University, and the recipient of fellowships from the Social Science Research Council and the MacArthur Foundation. She is a member of the International Advisory Board of the Institute on Disability and Public Policy (Bangkok) and the Asian Women Leadership University project. She has lived and worked in the Philippines, the US, the former Soviet Union and post-Soviet Russia, Hong Kong and Singapore. She has three children, aged 15, 10 and 2.

 **Kenneth Paul Tan** is an Associate Professor and Vice-Dean (Academic Affairs) of the Lee Kuan Yew School of Public Policy at the National University of Singapore, where he has taught since 2007. During this time, he has served as a member of the School's Management Committee, held administrative positions such as Assistant Dean (Academic Affairs) and Acting Director (Strategic Planning), and chaired a number of faculty committees. From 2000 to 2007, he taught at the University Scholars Programme and Political Science Department of the National University of Singapore (NUS), where he was Assistant Head from 2003 to 2005. Since 2000, he has received more than ten teaching awards, including the Outstanding Educator Award 2009, the highest teaching honour bestowed by NUS. He chairs the executive council of the NUS Teaching Academy and has served on the University Teaching Excellence Committee. Professor Tan has written widely about Singapore, mainly on (1) governance (focusing on meritocracy and pragmatism), democracy, and civil society; (2) the creative city and culture industry (focusing on film, television, and theatre); and (3) race, gender, and sexuality. He currently leads research projects on (1) nation/city branding and soft power (comparing Singapore and Finland); (2) spatial justice (comparing Singapore and Jakarta); and (3) Asian creative cities (comparing Singapore, Hong Kong, Seoul, and Taipei). He has published in leading international journals such as *Asian Studies*

Review, *Critical Asian Studies*, *International Political Science Review*, *Positions: Asia Critique*, and *PS: Political Science and Politics*, and has authored two books: *Renaissance Singapore? Economy, Culture, and Politics* (NUS Press, 2007) and *Cinema and Television in Singapore: Resistance in One Dimension* (Brill, 2008). He is also associate editor of *Asian Journal of Political Science*.

Professor Tan has held visiting fellowships at the Australian National University, Georgetown University (on a Fulbright Fellowship) and Harvard University. In 1995, he received a Lee Kuan Yew Postgraduate Scholarship to read for a PhD in social and political sciences at the University of Cambridge, which he completed in 2000. In 1994, he obtained a first-class honours degree in the joint school of economics and politics at the University of Bristol on a Public Service Commission Overseas Merit Scholarship (open).

Professor Tan is a member of the Arts Advisory Panel of the National Arts Council (Singapore). He is the founding chair of the Asian Film Archive's board of directors, sits on the board of directors of theatre company The Necessary Stage, and has composed music for some of its performances. He is married to Clara Lim-Tan, principal of Convent of the Holy Infant Jesus (Kellock).

Introduction
Inspiring Leaders, Improving Lives

Stavros N. Yiannouka

The pursuit of good governance has been a preoccupation of humanity at least since the time of Confucius and Socrates. For millennia, learned men and women from both East and West have been writing extensively on the role of the state and its relationship with the individual, in the process exploring such concepts as justice, equity and the pursuit of the good life. Many of these same political philosophers have also opined at length on how society should select its leaders and officeholders, and the qualities, skills and education required of them. And even though — most certainly in the case of Confucius and Socrates — their thinking originated in very different historical, political, economic and social contexts, most if not all political philosophers reached the same broad conclusions: that "the state came about as a means of securing life itself [and] it continues into being to secure the good life"[1] and that therefore the leaders and officeholders of state should "cultivate in [themselves] the capacity to ease the lot of the whole populace."[2] It is these very same objectives that are pithily encapsulated in the motto of the LKY School: *Inspiring Leaders, Improving Lives, Transforming Asia*.

The study of public administration and public policy at universities is an integral part of this millennia-old tradition and arguably represents the near universal acceptance of the belief that good governance can and should be both studied and

---

1   Aristotle (1981), *The Politics*, edited by Trevor J. Saunders and translated by T.A. Sinclair (Middlesex: Penguin Books), p. 59.

2   *The Analects of Confucius* (1992), edited by Jaroslav Pelikan and translated by Arthur Waley (United States of America: Quality Paperback), p. 191.

taught. The university-based study and teaching of public administration probably traces its origins to the efforts in the late 17ᵗʰ and early 18ᵗʰ Centuries of the largest German state, the Kingdom of Prussia,[3] to combat nepotism and corruption in its civil service. As part of his programme of reforms, the Prussian King, Frederick William I, established the first University Chairs for the study of the science of administration at the University of Halle and the University of Frankfurt an der Oder with the specific aim that they should train professional public administrators. In the mid to late 19ᵗʰ Century a German Professor, Lorenz von Stein, lecturing at the University of Vienna, established public administration as an interdisciplinary study that would be broadly recognisable today. Like a number of his Prussian predecessors, Lorenz von Stein was also involved in the practical applications of public administration theory when in the 1880s Japan's Meiji reformers consulted him on the drafting of the new Japanese constitution. One could also argue that Lorenz von Stein's influence over the Meiji reformation also underscored an early presumption that principles of good governance and public administration were transferable across borders.

By the mid-1930s the centre of gravity in the study of public administration began to shift away from Germany and towards the United States. The Great Depression of the 1930s, and the rise of totalitarian regimes in Germany and across much of Europe, is likely to have ignited interest in the study of good governance across the Atlantic Ocean. In 1930 Princeton University established its School of Public Affairs and in 1936 a Jewish-American football coach, businessman and politician named Lucius Nathan Littauer provided a USD2 million gift to his *alma mater* Harvard University to establish the Graduate School of Public Administration, which in 1966 was renamed the John F. Kennedy School of Government.

It was during the 1960s that the study of public administration was complemented by the introduction of public policy. While the discipline of public administration from its origins in Germany in the 19ᵗʰ Century to its transplantation in the United

---

3 Throughout most of its history, Germany was divided into a multitude of states of different shapes and sizes. The Kingdom of Prussia with its capital in Berlin was the largest and most powerful of these states and it was under its leadership that modern Germany was united in the period 1866–1870.

States in the 1930s was primarily concerned with the inner workings of government bureaucracies, the proponents of public policy education aspired to paint on a much broader canvass. The 1960s in the United States was the age of the "whiz kids" — the business leaders, academics and assorted policy wonks who were co-opted into public service by the Kennedy and Johnson administrations — many of whom believed that all challenges confronting governments, even war, could be solved using quantitative, analytical approaches.[4] It was during this time, therefore, that the study of economics, statistics and other quantitative analytical methods gained prominence in the new discipline of public policy. However, the 1960s was also a period of great and largely positive social change in the United States (and elsewhere) with the civil rights movement and the advent of the Great Society.[5] In this regard, therefore, the study of public policy also reflected interest in the big questions and challenges confronting society that many felt were not being addressed through the study of traditional public administration.

It is probably fair to deduce from the above brief history of the disciplines of public administration and public policy that both their origins and subsequent evolution coincided with periods of crisis, uncertainty and change; periods when people looked to governments for solutions to the great challenges of the day. At the turn of the 21st Century, the study of governance is potentially undergoing another significant transformation. Whilst for most of the 20th Century schools of public administration and public policy were largely concentrated in the United States, the early 21st Century has seen something of an explosion of such schools across Asia. Coupled with what could be described as the return of the discipline to Europe, the study of public policy and public administration is now a truly global endeavour. Not surprisingly, this new era in the study of public administration and policy is coinciding with a period of crisis (or crises even), uncertainty and great change. It has become *cliché* to say that the world is rapidly globalising and that our most intractable problems — from poverty to pandemics and global financial meltdown to

---

4   In his book *The Best and the Brightest* (New York: Random House, 1972), journalist David Halberstam makes a compelling case that the origins and conduct of the Vietnam War by the United States can be traced to the use and abuse of rational, analytical policy tools.

5   This was the name given to the set of policies introduced during the Johnson administration in the United States aimed at combating poverty and promoting racial equality.

global warming — are no longer confined within national boundaries, but an observation only becomes *clichéd* because it is true more often than not.[6] In addition to the numerous crises and challenges, the early 21st Century is also a period characterised by great (and by and large positive) changes particularly in the so-called developing world, primarily in Asia but increasingly elsewhere in the world too. As hundreds of millions of people are progressively lifted out of abject poverty particularly in Asia, the centre of gravity in world politics and the economy has decisively and perhaps irrevocably begun to shift from West to East.

It is against this broad historical backdrop that the Lee Kuan Yew School of Public Policy at the National University of Singapore came into being on 16 August 2004 following a decision by the Government of Singapore to create an institution of higher learning dedicated to the study and teaching of good governance, and bequeath it with the name of the widely-respected founder of modern Singapore. The aspiration was that the LKY School should over time "become a flagship institution, another peak of excellence within NUS... [and] be regarded globally as a reference point in public policy that can provide, through rigorous intellectual study, lessons on the principles and practices of good governance, particularly concerning Asian societies and the challenges of developing, transitional and newly industrialised economies."[7]

In the eight years that followed its establishment, the LKY School has gone a long way towards achieving the lofty aspirations set by its founders. Today the LKY School is widely recognised as a (if not the) preeminent school of public policy in Asia. In the chapters that follow, five members of the LKY School's faculty and management, including its founding Dean Kishore Mahbubani, share their perspectives and experience in helping to build and guide the School during its formative years.

---

6   For example, at the time of writing, the world is waiting anxiously to see whether politicians in Athens — the city where 2,500 years ago Socrates is believed to have first articulated his theories of governance — can form a government and prevent the economic crisis engulfing Greece from spiralling out of control and in the process potentially dragging Europe and the world into a second great depression.

7   Speech by Mr. Tharman Shanmugaratnam, then Minister for Education, at the launch of the Lee Kuan Yew School of Public Policy on Monday, 16 August 2004.

In Chapter 1, Professor Kishore Mahbubani shares his views as the founding Dean of the LKY School. He describes and analyses the reasons underlying the many successes of the School such as its early recognition by and acceptance into the global elite of public policy education; the successful launch and growth of the School's executive education business; and the remarkable ability of the School to attract significant funding support to the extent that it is now the third best-endowed school of public policy in the world after its peers at Harvard and Princeton. Beyond the successes of the School, Kishore also reflects on some of the longstanding challenges that confront not just the School but also its peers. For example he points out the fact that public policy and public administration are not settled disciplines with well-defined curricula and explains how this poses a significant conundrum for incumbent institutions but more so for new institutions when designing the curricula for their programmes. Kishore also reflects at length on the preponderance of what he describes as "Western social science" and discusses whether the School should be at the forefront of developing approaches to social science that are uniquely Asian.

In Chapter 2, I tell the story of how I came to be involved with the LKY School, initially through my work as a consultant with McKinsey & Company and subsequently by joining the School as the Vice-Dean tasked with implementing its growth strategy. I recount in some detail my experiences in helping, as a consultant, develop the LKY School's strategic blueprint and then driving its approach to branding and marketing for the purposes of student recruitment; building up its executive education business; and dealing with some of the challenges faced in building and managing the institution as a whole. Finally, I reflect on the lessons learnt about the nature of the academic enterprise and their implications for the future of the LKY School.

In Chapter 3, Professor Scott Fritzen provides an in-depth perspective on what he calls the three enigmas of professional policy education. He analyses in some detail the perennial and ever-present challenge of deciding what to teach and describes the three phases of curriculum development experienced by the LKY School. He then goes on to describe the inherent trade-offs involved in determining whom the LKY School should be teaching. He describes the School's admissions processes and the almost inevitable tensions encountered in selecting students from diverse geographic and socio-economic backgrounds. Finally, Scott addresses the third and final enigma of who should be doing the teaching and the need to strike the right balance in the faculty between academics and practitioners of public policy.

In Chapter 4, Dr. Astrid Tuminez addresses what is arguably the most significant challenge confronting a new school of public policy: namely, how to build a research community that generates output that is both academically rigorous and yet relevant in terms of the pertinent policy issues of the day. Drawing on her experiences working first as a researcher and subsequently as an executive in a foundation that provided funding for research, Astrid reflects on the achievements of the LKY School in research as well as the remaining challenges. Finally, Astrid provides her perspective on the themes that should inform the School's future research strategy and asks the tough question of whether the School has truly "arrived" as a generator of big ideas.

In the fifth and final chapter, Professor Kenneth Paul Tan reflects on the position of the School as a Singapore institution and its role in the codification and dissemination of Singapore's policy-making experiences. Specifically, he analyses the inherent tensions involved in the need for the School to engage the policy establishment in Singapore while at the same time maintaining the distance required to provide objective critiques of its policy practices. Citing extensively from his own work and that of other colleagues at the LKY School, Kenneth also addresses the question of whether or not the political environment in Singapore is conducive to the existence of a critically engaged school of public policy.

* * *

As noted by Kishore in the Preface, the book is not the most polished of products. It is part history and part reflective memoir and it contains both analysis and anecdote. Kishore is often fond of posing the question of whether public policy education is a sunrise or sunset industry. The brief history of philosophical enquiries into the nature of good governance and their subsequent evolution into the formal academic disciplines of public administration and policy, given at the beginning of this introduction, provides an answer of sorts. Public policy education is neither a sunrise nor a sunset industry. Rather, it is an evergreen industry because it addresses a question that is almost as old as human civilisation itself: namely, how best to organise and govern society. The LKY School is a very recent entrant into this age-old arena of academic inquiry. It has the aspiration and the resources to make a meaningful contribution to an endeavour that is ultimately designed to inspire leaders and improve lives.

1 Reflections of a Founding Dean

Kishore Mahbubani

It all began in New York.

Some time in 2003, the year Mr. Lee Kuan Yew turned 80, Dr. Tony Tan, then Deputy Prime Minister of Singapore and currently President of the Republic of Singapore, invited me for lunch at the Palace Hotel in New York. I was then serving as Singapore's Ambassador to the UN. At the lunch, Dr. Tan told me that the Singapore government would like me to consider becoming the founding Dean of a new School of Public Policy to be named after Mr. Lee Kuan Yew.

I accepted the invitation quite readily. I was then 55 years old and I knew that I would have to leave the Singapore Administrative Service within a few years. After having been Permanent Secretary of the Foreign Ministry and having represented Singapore at the UN Security Council, I was ready for a new challenge. And I had always wanted to go into academia. However, this ambition had to be shelved for 33 years, as the Foreign Service proved to be very exciting. Having finally joined academia, I am pleased to report that my eight years as Dean have been among the best and most satisfying years of my working life.

As the founding Dean, one of the few traditions I have started is to make three points in my speeches. Hence, this chapter will also have three parts. The first part answers the age-old question of who "owns" the LKY School. Here I will describe the contributions made by the many stakeholders to the School. The second part describes some of the key successes that the School has enjoyed in the academic, financial and executive education fields. The third part discusses the constant challenges that a public policy school faces and reflects on how the LKY School will respond to these challenges.

Who Owns the LKY School?

The LKY School has been blessed in many ways. One of our main blessings is the large variety of stakeholders, each of whom has made a significant contribution to the success of the School. I was alerted to this reality of many stakeholders when I was invited to a private dinner with my main "boss", then President of the NUS, Professor Shih Choon Fong, soon after I became Dean in August 2004.

We had a wonderful private dinner together. At the end of the dinner, Choon Fong gave me a copy of a famous book by the Harvard Dean, Professor Henry Rosovsky. The title was *The University: An Owner's Manual.* It was a truly fascinating book. Rosovsky, an excellent writer, described well the many stakeholders he encountered when he was the Dean of Harvard's Faculty of Arts and Sciences from 1973 to 1984. His book prepared me well for my new job because the LKY School proved to have even more stakeholders than those described in the book.

Mr. Lee Kuan Yew

The first and most obvious stakeholder was, of course, Mr. Lee Kuan Yew. It was very generous of him to share his name with our School. In subsequent years he also demonstrated his kind support in many other ways. However, he was always careful to not project his own ideas on the School. It was clear that he wanted the School to develop an independent reputation for excellence. While he always responded positively to our requests for support, he also wanted to give the School the space to grow and develop an independent identity. We have truly benefitted from this approach of his.

At the same time, Mr. Lee's support has been invaluable. At the very inception, he encouraged McKinsey to do a *pro bono* study to help the School's initial growth. Chapter 2 by Stavros Yiannouka explains well how we benefitted from this study. From time to time, Mr. Lee would also meet distinguished visitors hosted by the School, from Professor Roderick MacFarquhar and Professor David Ellwood of Harvard University to Mr. Paul Volcker, former Chairman of the Federal Reserve, who kindly agreed to become a member of our School's Governing Board. Also, as I will describe later in this chapter, Mr. Lee wrote an extremely important letter to Dr. Li Ka-shing, which resulted in a SGD100 million gift to our School. He also visited our School several times, gave several lectures and interacted with our students. For many of our students, this was one of the most valuable experiences of their time at the School. We were also truly blessed when he agreed to serve as a Distinguished Fellow when he retired from the Cabinet in May 2011.

The Singapore Government

The Singapore government has also proved to be a valuable stakeholder and supporter of our School. Like Mr. Lee Kuan Yew, the government provided discreet support without exercising any kind of heavy hand. We enjoyed academic freedom in developing our School. Then Minister for Defence and Minister in charge of the Civil Service, Mr. Teo Chee Hean, put it well when he received Professor David Ellwood, Dean of the Harvard Kennedy School, in his office on 27 March 2006. Minister Teo smiled broadly and told Professor Ellwood, "We have told Kishore that he should build the Lee Kuan Yew School of Public Policy and not the Lee Kuan Yew School of Thought." Minister Teo explained to Professor Ellwood that the LKY School provided an ideal opportunity for policy-makers to compare and contrast their respective experiences in governance and to study the best practices around the world, rather than focus on any specific theories. It was therefore important for the LKY School to be seen as an objective centre of academic research that commanded the respect of its peers. Professor Ellwood agreed with Minister Teo's observations. Clearly, this message had a powerful impact on Professor Ellwood and our friends in the Harvard Kennedy School (HKS).

Harvard Kennedy School

The HKS was another important stakeholder in our School. We were fortunate that we inherited the public policy programme that the HKS had set up in the National University of Singapore (NUS) in 1992. Hence, when we started the School in 2004, we did not have to start from scratch. We inherited a fully functioning Public Policy Programme with an established faculty, curriculum and tradition of recruiting good

Asian students. This programme initially began with an 18-month Master of Public Policy (MPP) with a class of 15 to 20 students. Later, in 2001, the NUS added a Master in Public Management (MPM) programme for more senior officials. This programme also had about 15 to 20 students. We have retained and expanded the MPP and MPM programmes, and further deepened and expanded the partnership with HKS.

One of the main contributions HKS has made to our School has been to send to us some of their distinguished faculty members to visit and lecture in our School. Most of the time, the faculty came to give lectures over a short period of time. We were therefore truly delighted when Professor Alan Altshuler, widely regarded to be one of the most insightful professors in Harvard, agreed to co-teach a course, "Singapore: The City", with Professor Kenneth Paul Tan during the second semesters of 2009 and 2010. In a similar way, we were also blessed when other equally eminent Professors like Robert Putnam and Steve Kelman agreed to serve as the Li Ka Shing Professor in our School in 2011 and 2012 respectively.

Our relations with HKS were helped a great deal by the fact that the Singapore Cabinet probably has more HKS graduates than any other Cabinet in the world. Mr. Lee Hsien Loong (Prime Minister), Mr. Teo Chee Hean (Deputy Prime Minister and Coordinating Minister for National Security and Minister for Home Affairs), Mr. Tharman Shanmugaratnam (Deputy Prime Minister and Minister for Finance and Minister for Manpower), Mr. Lim Hng Kiang (Minister for Trade and Industry), Mr. S. Iswaran (Minister, Prime Minister's Office and Second Minister for Home Affairs and Second Minister for Trade and Industry), and Mr. Heng Swee Keat (Minister for Education) are all graduates of HKS. David Ellwood, the HKS Dean, used to proudly tell me that when he travelled around the world, he would always mention PM Lee Hsien Loong as one of the outstanding graduates of HKS. Indeed, PM Lee set an unusual record for having co-published an article with Professor Richard Zeckhauser in a top-tier economic journal when PM Lee was only a student in Professor Zeckhauser's class.

In March 2010, PM Lee also agreed to post an article on our website to explain the virtues of public policy education. A few paragraphs are worth quoting here:

"My year as a Mason Fellow in the Harvard Kennedy School in 1979–80 confirmed my respect for the value of a public policy education. I picked up much from my fellow students, who came from all over the world. I learnt how economic principles were relevant to a wide range of public policy areas, even those which at first sight appeared far removed from economics. And I discovered how systematic, analytic thinking could clarify issues and suggest creative solutions to complex problems.

But my lasting lesson was that in a dynamic and demanding environment, public officers need more thorough preparation and effective tools for governance, to formulate policy rigorously and in depth, to evaluate trade-offs and develop mitigation measures, and crucially to garner political and public support to turn ideas into results.

This is especially relevant in Asia. Many Asian countries are transforming their economies, uplifting their peoples' lives and restructuring their bureaucracies. They seek to progress faster by learning from the experience of other countries which have gone ahead of them, to avoid making the same mistakes and to discover better ways forward.

The situation in each country is different, and public policies must adapt to the circumstances, needs and politics of each one. But good government is vital to progress everywhere. The rich range of experiences of Asian countries can be collected, compared, and analysed. These raw materials should be distilled into a coherent body of knowledge which public officers and scholars can tap on, and add to.

The LKY School is well-placed to play such a role. It is based in Singapore, which has paid particular attention to public policy and good government. It is also in the middle of Asia, where able, professional public officers are most needed to sustain the Asian miracle and to meet the challenges of globalisation and development. It attracts students from all over the world, and enjoys close links with outstanding public policy schools both in the East and West.

Preparing public officers to lead and serve their countries is a challenging but also a fulfilling mission. I am confident the LKY School will deliver to its students an outstanding public policy education, to provide them with the skills, knowledge and values to become agents of change and progress, within their workplaces, communities and countries." [1]

---

1   Lee Hsien Loong, "The Benefits of a Public Policy Education", 10 March 2010. Available at http://www.spp.nus.edu.sg/The_Benefits_of_a_Public_Policy_Education.aspx.

The PM would also regularly receive calls from distinguished HKS professors, such as David Ellwood and Robert Putnam. All this helped to cement our relationship with HKS. Indeed, as I was new to academia when I became Dean and as we were trying to build up the School rapidly, it helped the LKY School a lot to have this steady partnership with HKS. Members of the HKS faculty were generous in their time, advice and support as we put in place new programmes and processes in the School. I remember well a long one-to-one lunch I had with Professor David Ellwood in Davos. Similarly, I recall well a conversation I had with his predecessor, Professor Joseph Nye, also in Davos. As we were walking on snow and ice, I asked Joe Nye what the curriculum of a public policy school should consist of. He replied, "Kishore, it should rest on three pillars: Economics, Politics and Leadership and Management courses." I took his advice to heart. We also made it a point to consult our Harvard colleagues as we planned our new ventures. Like all partnerships, we had the usual ups and downs, but I am truly pleased to note here that over the years, the partnership has become stronger. In early 2012, a group of Young Global Leaders (YGLs) from the Davos World Economic Forum called on the new Academic Dean of HKS, Iris Bohnet. They asked her whether HKS had developed partnerships with other institutions. A Young Global Leader who was attending the meeting was pleased that she mentioned the LKY School as an important partner of HKS.

The Students

When I began reading Henry Rosovsky's *The University: An Owner's Manual*, I fully expected him to put the President and Governing Board of Harvard *first* as the owners of Harvard University. Instead, he put them last. He placed the students first. After eight years as Dean, I have realised the wisdom of his judgement.

The most important stakeholders of any academic institution are the students. They give up valuable years of their lives when they join a school of public policy like ours. If we do not add value to them when they are with us, we will have failed in our mission. Fortunately, the School has received many testimonials from its students saying that the LKY School has added value to their lives.

As Dean, I have two important formal encounters with every batch of students. The first encounter is at the opening orientation session. It is truly moving to see the enthusiasm with which they begin their studies. The second encounter is at the closing valedictory dinners. These valedictory dinners are important occasions as few of our overseas students (who make up the majority of the student population) return for the official graduation ceremonies a year later. Hence, these valedictory dinners provide them with the opportunity to bid farewell to the LKY School.

The students could leave the LKY School feeling tired or burnt out from their stay in our School. Instead, these valedictory dinners are full of excitement and enthusiasm as they speak about their student experience at the LKY School, and show videos and slides commemorating their time at the School. What comes through unfailingly at each valedictory dinner is their overwhelming happiness with their experience in our School. Indeed, these valedictory dinners became so celebratory that we finally decided to dispense with the time-honoured tradition of having distinguished Guests-of-Honour at such dinners. We found that the presence of these distinguished guests actually dampened the enthusiastic spirits of these dinners and took away from the evening of fun and reflection that the students wanted to have. Looking back now, I wish that we had videotaped some of these events. They would have provided eloquent testimonials of how the LKY School has enriched the lives of these students.

When the students reflect on their experiences, it is clear that they have learnt a lot from formal teaching in the classrooms. From time to time, they would pay tribute to their professors. The graduating MPP class of 2012, for example, started a new practice of giving out Oscar-style awards to the faculty. They gave out the following awards:

1) Dr. Suzaina Kadir — Most Caring Professor
2) Visiting Professor Thampapillai J. Dodo — Most Memorable Professor
3) Visiting Associate Professor Razeen Sally — Coolest Professor
4) Associate Professor Kenneth Paul Tan — Most Engaging Professor
5) Associate Professor Kenneth Paul Tan — Most Inspiring Professor (Core Modules)

6) Professor Huang Jing — Most Inspiring Professor (Elective Modules)

7) Professor Charles Adams — Most Inspiring Professor (Elective Modules)

To give out these teaching awards was a purely spontaneous decision of the students, with no prompting at all by the School administration or faculty. Such spontaneous tributes are among the most valuable that a School can receive.

When they speak about their experience at the LKY School, the students also speak without fail about what they learnt from each other. We probably provide some of the most diverse public policy classrooms in the entire world. The students say that when they discuss a specific public policy problem, they are astonished to discover how different their perspectives can be from students of different countries. They absorb and understand the real diversity of our world almost through a process of osmosis. In so doing, the School may be providing the students with a strong competitive asset for their future careers as they leave the School with a high degree of cultural sensitivity that is a huge asset in an increasingly globalised world. In addition, the strong regional and global networks that have developed in our School can also contribute over the longer run to increase international understanding and cooperation. These are the other intangible benefits provided by an education at the LKY School.

At the same time, there has also been cross-cultural misunderstanding in our School. I recall vividly one painful experience that the LKY School had. Some students from China were upset that in the process of discussing a case study from China, some of the "failures" of that case were also discussed. The students regarded that as a national insult and protested vigorously. We had to carefully and patiently explain to them that their role at the LKY School was not to serve as ambassadors of their country but as students. Students can only learn from critical enquiry and questioning. Indeed, we emphasised that they would be more valuable to their country if they could dissect and learn from their country's failures as much as their successes. In subsequent years, I made it a point to emphasise to all incoming classes that they should act not as ambassadors but as critics of their own countries in classrooms.

The other heartening aspect of the LKY School's student community is the independent initiatives that the students have taken on their own volition. Without much prodding from the School, they set up their own journal, called the *Asian Journal of Public Affairs* (AJPA). So far, the students have produced eight issues of the journal. I was surprised that they were able to maintain continuity of production since the majority of our students spend only one or two years in our School. Hence, each class has had little contact with subsequent classes, unlike undergraduate and PhD students who might spend several years with an institution.

The myriad of student initiatives included donation drives. For example, in October 2006, Aziz Tyebally, valedictorian of the MPA class of 2006–2007, organised a blood donation drive with the Singapore Red Cross. In September 2009, 14 Filipino MPP students organised a donation drive and an interfaith service in memory of the victims of the 2009 Philippine floods. In January 2010, students from the MPP, MPA and MPM organised a donation drive for victims of the 2010 Haiti earthquake. In August 2010, Denise Tan from the MPP class of 2010–2012 launched a donation drive for the victims of floods in Pakistan. In March 2011, after an earthquake struck Japan, a group of the School's Japanese students worked with Singaporean students from the NUS Law School to organise a collaborative donation drive at the Bukit Timah Campus.

Sports initiatives were also launched. For instance, the MPP class of 2005–2006 formed an LKY School soccer team which went on to participate in the NUS tournaments. The LKY School soccer team exists till this day. In January 2007, Zhang Kejie of the MPP class of 2006–2008 also launched a weekly Sports Day initiative on Friday afternoons featuring basketball, volleyball, badminton, tennis and squash.

I have been particularly impressed by the study tours organised by our students. In June 2010, after the enterprising efforts of Geng Jing, an MPM student, the organisers of the Shanghai Expo 2010 invited the MPM class of 2009–2010 to Shanghai to attend the Expo and sponsored the participants' local expenses over a four-day period. In June 2012, an MPM student, Kim Rithy, organised a 5-day study trip to Cambodia for his class. The theme of the study trip was "The Quest for Peace, Security, and Economic Development: The Cambodian Experience". During the trip, they met chief Cambodian policy-makers in order to understand Cambodia's experience and ongoing efforts towards national reconstruction and reconciliation, providing public infrastructure and services and promoting economic development.

Here is how one MPM student, Elaine Leh, described the trip: "It was an exceptional learning experience — essentially a crash course on more than a thousand years of Cambodian history — which left us in awe (of the Angkor empire), in horror (of the Pol Pot-era genocide) but more importantly, in anticipation and hope for Cambodia's future development."

In February 2011, Daisuke Asano and Kenichi Tanaka, two MPA students of the class of 2010–2011, organised a one-week study trip to Japan. This was then followed by the initiative of a double-degree Japanese student, Shumpei Watanabe, to independently raise money from the Japan Foundation and the Japan Chamber of Commerce and Industry. Shumpei led a team of students to raise the staggering sum of SGD160,000 to fund a visit to Japan in February 2012. 45 students and faculty members from the MPA, MPP and PhD programmes in the School participated in the trip. The visit was remarkably successful and at the end they published a rich volume full of coloured photographs, which actually may look more impressive than this slim volume of 8th anniversary reflections. It is a great tribute to our School that a student publication can outshine an official publication of the School.

What makes this support of the Japanese government agencies even more remarkable is that in the early years of the LKY School, we had great difficulty attracting young Japanese or young Japanese public servants to come and study in our School. I made several visits to Tokyo to try to persuade Japanese government ministries to send students to our School. My initial efforts failed as I ran into some strong bureaucratic opposition. The Japanese bureaucrats explained to me politely and patiently that for their English language Master's programmes, they sent their students to English-speaking countries like the US and UK, Australia and Canada. Since they were of the view that Singapore was not an English-speaking country, they could not send students to the LKY School. Fortunately, we were able to persuade the Japanese government otherwise over time. Now with the help of our graduates from Japan, this misconception about the use of English in Singapore has been rectified.

This deep sense of student "ownership" of the LKY School is probably one of the strongest features of our School. Such ownership does not happen by accident.

It is a result of the enormous support provided to them by our programme officers.[2] It is also a result of the support from the faculty and the wonderful environment provided by College Green.

The contribution of "bricks and mortar" to the success of an institution is often underrated. There is no doubt that the Bukit Timah Campus (BTC) we inherited in 2006 is one of the most beautiful campuses in Asia. Built in the 1920s on a piece of land donated by the Straits Settlement government, BTC was the campus ground for Raffles College, a college for higher education in the arts and sciences. The original design of the campus was by Cyril Farey and Graham Dawbam of London and it was the winning design of the British empire-wide architectural competition in 1922. Since I studied in BTC from 1967 to 1971, I have firsthand experience of how the personal beauty of the campus can enhance the student experience. I did not stay in College Green (which was then known as the Dunearn Road Hostels). However, all the students who used to stay there, including former President S.R. Nathan and Chairman of our Governing Board Professor Wang Gungwu, confirm that it provides a wonderful living environment. And whenever I travel around the world meeting the *alumni* of the LKY School, they always emphasise how much they miss College Green. All this has significantly enhanced the bonding between students and the School, making them among the proudest "owners" of the School.

The Faculty

"Bricks and Mortar" may also be one reason why the faculty of the LKY School are attached to the School. This is not unique to the LKY School. Henry Rosovsky describes the "faculty" in his book as the second set of owners of a university. He begins his chapter by trying to explain why "professors of good universities have a much more positive attitude towards their work". And what was his answer? "One reason may be that most of our colleges and universities are physically attractive. The very notion of campus evolves in our minds a picture of dress, lawns and imposing structures."[3] The LKY School is blessed with all these elements.

---

2   Agnes Tan, Associate Director (MPA and MPM programmes), Wendy Tan, Assistant Manager (MPA Programme) and Ruth Choe, formerly Associate Director (External Affairs).

3   Henry Rosovsky (1990), *The University: An Owner's Manual* (Norton), p. 160.

This may be one reason why the faculty of the LKY School feels a deep sense of ownership of the School. However, an equally important source of "ownership" of the School may be the "nobility" of the mission of the School. Here let me emphasise that the academic calling is an inherently noble profession. Rosovsky also explains why faculties develop a deep sense of ownership of their institutions: "The formal duties imposed by our institutions are minimal, anywhere between six and twelve hours in the classroom per week during eight months of the year. Yet most of us work long hours and spend many evenings at our desks or in our laboratories. We do not tell students that this is our day off, that they must seek someone else with whom to discuss their problems. We do practice our profession as a calling, considering ourselves not employees but shareholders of the university: a group of owners."[4]

The mission of the LKY School may be even nobler than most other academic institutions because we try to select and educate students who believe in public service. The nobility of this mission is indeed captured in our mission statement: *Inspiring Leaders, Improving Lives, Transforming Asia.* At the end of the day, when a professor has both educated a student and inspired him to do more with his knowledge, he or she has made a significant contribution to making the world a better place. Not many professions have such nobility of purpose.

This nobility may provide at least one explanation of why the LKY School has been blessed with a collegial faculty. I am not giving away any secrets in saying that faculties are not necessarily collegial. Henry Kissinger was known to quote Wallace Sayre as saying that "academic politics is the most vicious and bitter form of politics, because the stakes are so low".[5] Indeed, one reason why I became slightly disenchanted with academia in 1975 is because I discovered as a graduate student in Dalhousie University that academic politics was in some ways worse than the bureaucratic politics that I experienced in the Singapore Foreign Service.

It would be *naïve* to pretend that the LKY School faculty is totally devoid of academic politics. Indeed, some degree of rivalry can be healthy in an organisation.

---

4   *Ibid.*, p. 165.

5   Quoted in *The Wall Street Journal*, 20 December 1973.

However, the LKY School is blessed that any such rivalry has not led to the creation of any kinds of cliques or factions in the School. Instead, as the chapters by Scott Fritzen, Astrid Tuminez and Kenneth Paul Tan will show, there has been an unusually high degree of collaboration and cooperation among the LKY School faculty. This has been a true blessing for the School.

The enthusiasm of the faculty of the LKY School may also explain the enthusiasm of the students of the LKY School that I described earlier. Indeed, when I meet the *alumni* of our School, they speak with great wonderment of the amount of time that faculty members had spent with them in and outside the classroom. Many of our faculty members do not even post "office hours" for student consultation. They welcome the students and keep their offices open. Some of them even meet the students during weekends.

Professor Asit Biswas is a distinguished visiting professor at the LKY School. Yet, when he teaches a course, he works very closely with his students. As a result, many of his students have had their essays published in academic journals as he strongly encourages them to do so. For example, an entire issue of the *International Journal of Water Resources Development* contained the work of the students of Professor Asit Biswas and Professor Cecilia Tortajada. It was so well received that Routledge decided to publish this special issue as a book under the title *Asian Perspectives on Water Policy*. Other than Professor Biswas and Professor Tortajada's papers, all the other papers were by their students.

In addition, one of Professor Biswas' doctoral students, Leong Ching, has worked with Professor Biswas on a number of op-eds which have been published in several newspapers including the *International Herald Tribune*, *The Straits Times*, *The Business Times* and *The Jakarta Post*.

Governance

The final section of Rosovsky's volume on *The University: An Owner's Manual* is devoted to "governance". One unique aspect of the LKY School is that it is accountable to both the NUS and to an independent Governing Board. The Charter of the LKY School states explicitly this dual accountability in Clause 13 (1):

13. (1) The Dean shall report:

(a) to the Governing Board on matters involving strategic planning, finance and development of the School; and

(b) through the Provost to the President on academic and research matters, including academic personnel, subject to the provisions of this Charter.

One real blessing that the LKY School has enjoyed is the strong support from both the NUS and the Governing Board. Both President Shih Choon Fong and his equally distinguished successor, Professor Tan Chorh Chuan, have been strongly supportive of the LKY School. Here again, it is worth emphasising that harmony between schools and the central administration of a university is not a natural phenomenon. To make matters even more complicated, the LKY School enjoys a significant amount of "autonomy" from the NUS. Indeed, it probably enjoys far more "autonomy" than any other NUS institution. This autonomy was carved out for the School by an important Steering Committee that was set up to establish the School. It was headed by Mr. Lim Siong Guan, then head of Civil Service, and reported to Dr. Tony Tan, then Deputy Prime Minister, Rear-Admiral Teo Chee Hean, then Minister for Defence, and Mr. Tharman Shanmugaratnam, then Acting Minister for Education.

This autonomy would have generated tension between the School and the NUS. Wise stewardship has minimised any such tension. Professor Shih Choon Fong confided in me that the NUS was happy to give the new LKY School the maximum amount of autonomy within the NUS as he viewed the LKY School as an experiment. If the School succeeded with its autonomy, it could then provide a model for other institutions within the NUS. This may well provide one useful reason for the publication of this book. We hope that it will help to demonstrate that providing more autonomy within universities may well help to allow schools to develop successfully.

To ensure that this autonomy was exercised responsibly, the NUS also set up a high-level Governing Board to oversee the activities of the School. One of the blessings that the School has enjoyed has been the constant and strong support from the Chairman of the Board, Professor Wang Gungwu. Indeed, it is hard to imagine how the School could have had a better Chairman than Professor Wang. He too had studied in the Bukit Timah Campus from 1949 to 1955. This emotional connection, both with the campus and College Green, where he stayed, runs deep. After a truly distinguished academic career in the former Malaya, Australia and Hong Kong (where he served as Vice-Chancellor of the University of Hong Kong from 1986 to 1995), he returned to Singapore to become the Chairman of the East Asian Institute from 1997 to 2007.

Professor Wang has been an unfailing source of support for the School in many ways. The twice-yearly meetings of the Governing Board that he chairs are only one part of the contribution. He also provides a constant stream of informal advice and assistance on many sensitive issues. He also chairs the selection committee for the Li Ka Shing Professorship. He always makes an effort to attend as many School functions as he can. He has possibly attended more lectures and seminars of our School than any of our own faculty members have. He often lunches at the student canteen and is seen either with a book as companion or engaged in conversation with a student or faculty member. This public show of support has been heartwarming for both the students and the faculty of the School. In addition, he and his wife, Margaret Wang, also make it a point to attend the valedictory dinners and other important ceremonial occasions of the School as often as they can. Clearly Professor Wang has been a constant pillar of support and a key stakeholder of the LKY School. As someone who is very approachable, kind and always shows appreciation to staff and faculty, Professor Wang has endeared himself greatly to the staff, faculty and students of the School.

Professor Wang's distinguished chairmanship also enabled the School to attract luminaries from Singapore and overseas to serve on the Governing Board. I recall vividly how surprised many observers were when Mr. Paul Volcker, the former Chairman of the US Federal Reserve, agreed to become a member of our Governing Board on 1 April 2006. It created a big news splash and the local business paper, *The Business Times*, made it front cover headline news with an almost full-page photo of the very tall Paul Volcker.[6] In addition to attending the Governing Board

---

6   Conrad Tan, "Former Fed chief Volcker to join LKY School board", *Business Times*, 24 March 2006.

meeting, Mr. Volcker has also delivered several public lectures to our School to sell-out crowds. All this helped to significantly enhance the stature of the School in Singapore and in the world.

Paul Volcker is not the only international luminary to agree to serve on our Board. Others include Viktor Halberstadt, former President of the International Institute of Public Finance and currently Professor of Economics at Leiden University, The Netherlands; Mr. Toyoo Gyohten, President of the Institute for International Monetary Affairs and a former Chairman of the Bank of Tokyo; and Ambassador Susan Schwab, the former United States Trade Representative. Most recently, Her Excellency Sheikha Lubna bint Khalid bin Sultan Al Qasimi, the UAE's Minister of Foreign Trade, joined our Board on 1 May 2012.

The Board has also been blessed with equally strong support from Singapore luminaries. It would not be fair to mention a few and not the rest. Let me list out the names of all who have served on our Board. They are Professor Wang Gungwu; Mr. Peter Ho and Mr. Peter Ong (Heads of the Civil Service); Mr. Eddie Teo, Mr. Chiang Chie Foo and Mr. Benny Lim (Permanent Secretaries in the Prime Minister's Office); Mr. Wong Ah Long (Chairman of Pacific Star Investment and Development); Mr. Lee Tzu Yang (Chairman of Shell Companies in Singapore); Mr. Phillip Tan Eng Seong (Director of EQ Insurance Company Limited); Professor Shih Choon Fong and Professor Tan Chorh Chuan (former and current Presidents of the NUS); Professor Cham Tao Soon (founding President of Nanyang Technological Institute); Professor Tommy Koh, Mr. Lee Hsien Yang (Chairman of Fraser and Neave Limited); Mr. Philip Ng (Chief Executive Officer of Far East Organization); Dr. Teh Kok Peng (Advisor to the Group Executive Committee of the Government of Singapore Investment Corporation); Mr. Lim Chee Onn (Senior International Advisor to Singbridge Pte Ltd); Professor Lim Pin (former Vice-Chancellor of the NUS); Mr. Koh Boon Hwee (Chairman of Sunningdale Tech Ltd and Yeo Hiap Seng Ltd) and Ms. Kwa Kim Li (Managing Partner, Lee & Lee).

Even though I said in the above paragraph that it would not be fair to mention only a few names, I am going to break my own commitment by mentioning one name from the above list who has played a special role in our School. This person is the legendary Professor Tommy Koh. He has long been a close personal friend of mine as I had to step into his shoes as the Singapore Ambassador to the UN in August 1984. Since then, we have worked closely in the Foreign Service and elsewhere.

Tommy Koh played an unusually important role for the School when the LKY School was asked to take on board one of the most eminent local think-tanks, the Institute of Policy Studies (IPS) in 2007. The IPS has always been close to the heart of Tommy Koh as he has served as Director of IPS from 1990 to 1997 and from December 2000 to July 2004. He is currently Special Advisor of the IPS. At the very first meeting between the staff of the LKY School and the IPS, after the IPS had moved to the Bukit Timah Campus, Tommy and I joked publicly that both the LKY School and the IPS had had a traditional Asian "arranged marriage". In Western marriages, couples fall in love and then get married. In Asian arranged marriages, couples marry and then fall in love. Both of us declared that the LKY School and IPS would fall in love after the arranged marriage. So far, it has been a happy arranged marriage because of the strong support from Tommy Koh and the two distinguished IPS Directors, Ambassador Ong Keng Yong and Mr. Janadas Devan.

I could go on and mention many more names of outstanding individuals who have helped or supported the School. But I will stop here as the only message I wish to convey in this section is a simple one: The success of any institution is not the result of a single person or a single group of people. The success of the LKY School is a result of the tremendous contributions made by multiple groups of stakeholders: from the students to the faculty, from Mr. Lee Kuan Yew to the Harvard Kennedy School. And as this volume will amply demonstrate, there have been many other important supporters and stakeholders. Hence, this is an appropriate moment to transition into the next section where we discuss the notable achievements of the LKY School.

Notable Achievements of the LKY School

Academic Achievements

As an academic institution, the most important assessment of our School has to come from our academic peers. Without their support and encouragement, we could not possibly claim to have achieved success in our mission. And academic endorsement does not come easily. Indeed, this is one of the key paradoxes of working in the academic world, especially in the world of leading Western academic institutions. On the one hand, academics know that in the world of ideas, academic collaboration produces better results. On the other hand, academic institutions tend to compete more than collaborate. Indeed, some of the leading academic institutions, like Harvard and Yale, are so keen to preserve their unique branding that they almost never agree to double degrees because a double degree would signify that the degrees of two institutions have equal academic value.

Given this inherent difficulty in signing double-degree agreements with leading academic institutions, one of the most remarkable achievements of the Lee Kuan Yew School of Public Policy is that we were able to sign double-degree agreements with three leading global institutions: the School of International and Public Affairs (SIPA) of Columbia University, the London School of Economics (LSE) and the Paris Institute of Political Studies (Sciences Po) within three years of our establishment. We worked hard on securing these double degrees as it was an implicit condition for admission into the exclusive Global Public Policy Network (GPPN).

In Chapter 2, Stavros describes how we joined the GPPN. Clearly one of the big achievements of our School is that we gained admission in June 2007 barely three years after our establishment. As a result, we were able to host a significant GPPN conference in our School in October 2007. Eminent luminaries like Professor Mario Monti (currently Prime Minister of Italy), Sir Howard Davies, Mr. Richard Descoings (now sadly deceased) and Professor Anne-Marie Slaughter participated in this conference.

So why did the School gain such positive academic peer recognition so soon after its establishment? Several people and institutions deserve credit for this. Firstly, it helped enormously that our School had inherited a credible Public Policy Programme (PPP) which had been set up in collaboration with Harvard University's Kennedy School of Government (HKS) in 1992. This collaboration with the HKS continued even after we became a School. The HKS Dean, Professor David Ellwood, came to Singapore to personally sign the extension of the agreement on 29 March 2006. Eminent Harvard professors like Professor Robert Putman, Professor Alan Altshuler,

Professor Steve Kelman and others have visited and lectured in our School. We were particularly happy that one of the former teachers of Prime Minister Lee Hsien Loong in HKS, Professor Richard Zeckhauser, visited Singapore in March 2008 as a Lee Kuan Yew Distinguished Visitor. These eminent academic visitors added academic lustre to our School.

Secondly, it also helped enormously that the LKY School was part of the National University of Singapore (NUS). I came to discover the global standing of the NUS when I was invited to attend the Global University Leaders Forum (GULF) set up by the Davos World Economic Forum (WEF). GULF comprised of a select group of university presidents (from universities such as Harvard, Yale, Columbia, U Penn, Oxford and Cambridge) and two university deans, the HKS Dean David Ellwood and myself. Initially, this group was co-led by Professor Larry Summers (then President of Harvard) and Professor Richard Levin (President of Yale). However, when Larry Summers stepped down as President of Harvard, I was asked to step into his place and be the co-convenor of GULF with Richard Levin. This exposure to the top university heads in the world also proved to be an asset to the LKY School and the NUS. A few years later, I resigned from GULF and WEF invited President Tan Chorh Chuan to become a member. All these symbolised the high global standing that the NUS enjoyed in the eyes of its peers.

Thirdly, it helped a lot that our School started with a base of strong faculty members, many of whom had been recruited before the School began. Without this strong base, our academic programmes would not have passed muster in the eyes of our colleagues at peer institutions. Indeed, several faculty members from SIPA, Columbia University, came to Singapore to attend and audit our programmes before recommending to the Columbia University Senate to sign a double-degree programme with us. When I started out as Dean in 2004, I knew that given my relative inexperience in the academic universe, I had to start with a strong Vice-Dean (Academic Affairs). Fortunately, after some persuasion, Associate Professor Hui Weng Tat from the Economics Department agreed to join us. It helped that he had previously been associated with our predecessor Public Policy Programme and he knew well our HKS colleagues like Professor John Thomas. As the founding

Vice-Dean (Academic Affairs), Weng Tat put in place various academic processes and standards that have passed the test of time and done the School proud.

When our School started, we had only two tenured faculty members, Professor Mukul Asher and Associate Professor Hui Weng Tat. I am proud to report that since then several faculty members have gained tenure in our School: Professor M. Ramesh, Associate Professor Scott Fritzen, Associate Professor Wu Xun, Associate Professor Kenneth Paul Tan and Associate Professor Darryl Jarvis. We also recruited another tenured member of the NUS, Associate Professor Phua Kai Hong. For a small School, this is truly an impressive track record, especially given the high standards that NUS has set for tenured positions. This strong faculty base has proved to be a major asset for our School. And this base has been further enhanced with other "senior" hires like Professor Jeff Straussman, former Dean of the Rockefeller College of Public Affairs and Policy, University at Albany–SUNY, Professor Huang Jing of the Brookings Institution and Professor Kanti Bajpai of Oxford University. Other distinguished scholars who have spent a year or more at our School include Professor T.N. Srinivasan, the inaugural Yong Pung How Chair Professor, Professor Ann Florini, the inaugural Director of the Centre for Asia and Globalisation, Associate Professor Viktor Mayer-Schönberger and Visiting Professor Lee Chung Min.

On the 8th anniversary of the School, it is particularly apt to report that the School has recruited a bumper crop of young academics in 2012. Academic institutions, like other institutions, benefit from a healthy influx of young blood. And, given our location in Singapore, far off the beaten track as far as US-trained PhDs are concerned, it has not been easy to recruit young scholars graduating from leading universities. Therefore, the recent recruitment of some outstanding academics provides another strong testimonial of how well the School is doing in the eyes of the academic community. And for this recruitment success, we need to pay special tribute to Professor Jeff Straussman who led this exercise.

Let me, as a significant aside, mention that the School is succeeding in both recruiting and producing top PhD students. Here, I must confess that as the founding Dean I was reluctant to expand the small PhD programme at the School as I was afraid that we would not be able to find jobs for our PhD graduates. This would have clearly damaged the standing of our School. Fortunately, my fears proved groundless. As Scott notes in Chapter 3, all the PhD graduates of our School have found employment immediately.

One of the inherent contradictions about an academic career in a school of public policy is that while the mission of the academics in the School is to teach and prepare future policy-makers in the practical world, their own standing in the academic world comes from their contributions to academic journals. This built-in tension affects all public policy schools, as I will discuss later in this chapter. Nevertheless, it is worth noting that our faculty have done well in their academic research. Chapter 4 by Astrid provides some good statistics on how our research record has improved over the years.

The biggest compliment to our faculty comes, ironically, when other institutions try to "steal" them. So, paradoxically, when an academic institution "loses" faculty, it may actually be winning as it demonstrates that it has been able to recruit excellent faculty. Hence, it was a compliment to our School that Visiting Professor Lee Chung Min went on to become Dean and Professor of International Relations, Graduate School of International Studies, Yonsei University, Korea and Associate Professor Viktor Mayer-Schönberger became Professor of Internet Governance and Regulation at the Oxford Internet Institute, University of Oxford. In addition, Dr. Seetharam, whom we borrowed from ADB to run our Institute of Water Policy, was chosen by the NUS to be the first Director of the Global Asian Institute. We have also loaned Associate Professor Scott Fritzen for two years to serve as Associate Dean at New York University's Robert F. Wagner Graduate School of Public Service from August 2012. Associate Professor Darryl Jarvis has accepted an invitation to become Professor and Associate Dean of Research and Post Graduate Studies at the Hong Kong Institute of Education. Stavros Yiannouka will join the Qatar Foundation as CEO of the World Innovation Summit for Education. It is always good for a School when its faculty are in high demand.

Financial Standing

The second big achievement of our School is financial. It is truly astonishing that even though we are only eight years old, we have become the third-best endowed

School of Public Policy in the world. The best endowed is the Harvard Kennedy School with USD1.1 billion for 1,062 students. The second-best endowed is the Woodrow Wilson School of Princeton University with USD900 million for 200 students. The third-best endowed is the Lee Kuan Yew School with USD270 million (when all the pledges come in) for 300 students.

There is one simple reason why we have become the third-best endowed School in the world. It is due to the fact that we are called the "Lee Kuan Yew" School. There is enormous respect and regard for Mr. Lee both in Singapore and in the Asia-Pacific region. Several donors have given money to the School as a gesture of respect for Mr. Lee. The fund-raising began early and, indeed, started at his 80th birthday party. Prime Minister Goh Chok Tong and his Cabinet worked hard to raise money. Mr. Lim Boon Heng was put in charge. He made direct phone calls to many. As a result, SGD67 million was raised, of which SGD4 million was used for a Discovery Channel documentary on Singapore.

Just before I assumed the deanship, I had another meeting with then DPM Dr. Tony Tan. Using some back-of-the-envelope calculations, he explained to me how the School would have access to a SGD200 million budget over the first ten years, including SGD6.3 million per year from Mr. Lee Kuan Yew's birthday party funds. Hence, by the end of the seventh year, we were expected to have spent 7 × SGD6.3 million (or SGD44.1 million). I am pleased to report here that as a result of the prudent financial management of the School, we have retained about SGD50 million of the birthday funds. This money serves as a useful buffer for us to use on "rainy days". Indeed, this is what we did when the 2008–2009 financial crisis hit our endowment fund badly. The NUS also generously loaned us some money to tide us over a difficult period. We have since repaid all the NUS loans.

The best indicator of the respect and regard that Mr. Lee enjoys in this region came in January 2007 when I called on Dr. Li Ka-shing with a brief three-paragraph letter from Mr. Lee. The first paragraph introduced me and provided my background. The second paragraph explained that the School had just moved to the historic Bukit Timah Campus. Two buildings were named. One was not. The School hoped to name a building after Dr. Li. In the third paragraph, Mr. Lee expressed the hope that Dr. Li would make an appropriate contribution.

I had called on Dr. Li Ka-shing with our then Consul-General in Hong Kong, Ambassador Toh Hock Ghim. Indeed we were received very warmly by Dr. Li and his assistant, Ms. Amy Au, because Ambassador Toh had also developed a close friendship with Dr. Li. When we went for the meeting, Dr. Li Ka-shing agreed to our proposed amount of SGD100 million and we were truly delighted. It was clearly one of the happiest days of my life. And we informed Mr. Lee Kuan Yew immediately of this generous gift by Dr. Li, which we agreed would be provided to the School over ten years.

This generous gift from Dr. Li and the matching 1-to-1 grant from the Singapore government explains well how we have become the third-best endowed School of Public Policy in the world. In addition, we have also raised money at significant anniversaries of the School. At the 5th anniversary of the School, for example, we set ourselves a very modest target of raising SGD5 million. Since the government provided matching 1-to-1 grants, we had to raise only SGD2.5 million. We were truly fortunate that both the Chairman of the NUS Board of Trustees, Mr. Wong Ngit Liong, and the President of the NUS, Professor Tan Chorh Chuan, decided to help us with our fund-raising efforts. They hosted a series of lunches and meetings for us to meet prospective donors. As a result, instead of raising SGD2.5 million, we raised SGD16.5 million, which meant a total contribution of SGD33 million to our School. This amount was 50 percent of what was raised at Mr. Lee Kuan Yew's 80th birthday party. The major donors included Mr. Kuok Khoon Hong, Mr. Martua Sitorus, Mr. Wong Fong Fui, Mr. Tay Liam Wee, Mr. Chang Yung-fa, Dr. B.K. Modi, Mr. Murli Chanrai and Mr. Ow Chio Kiat.

Amazingly, we were able to raise funds even during difficult times. In 2007, the price of AIG shares fell sharply. Mr. Oei Hong Leong bought a million shares at USD1.80 each on 16 September 2008, the 85th birthday of then Minister Mentor Lee Kuan Yew. On 22 September, he sold them at USD5 each. He donated the entire sum of SGD7 million to the Lee Kuan Yew School, remarking, "Under MM Lee's leadership, we have a clean and efficient Government."[7]

---

7   "Oei's perfect timing nets $7m", *The Straits Times*, p. A47, 8 October 2008. Available at http://new-shub.nus.edu.sg/news/0810/PDF/PERFECT-st-8Oct-pA7.pdf.

All the funds we have collected for the endowment fund are invested by the NUS Investment Office. In return, we get a payout of approximately 4 percent a year from the endowment fund. Hence, when our endowment fund approaches USD300 million, we should get a guaranteed base of USD12 million a year (or over SGD15 million of income per year). This will provide a healthy financial base for the School over the long term.

The gift of the "Lee Kuan Yew" name was, of course, the primary reason why the School succeeded in becoming the third-best endowed School of Public Policy in the world. However, it also helped that those who contributed money to the School knew that they were supporting both a noble and a worthwhile cause. Education in itself is always a noble cause. However, the School also has another noble mission: educating the next generation of Asian leaders. We were acutely aware when we started the School that many Asian societies were on the right economic track. The big challenge they faced was whether they could develop the strong political, social and administrative institutions to keep this economic growth going. Hence, if our School succeeds in its mission of producing capable, committed and ethical leaders, who in turn help their societies, our School could eventually improve the lives of millions, if not hundreds of millions, of people. This noble mission also helped us to raise money for the School.

As I noted in my remarks at the School's 5th Anniversary Gala Dinner, a School of Public Policy is a much more expensive operation than any other professional school. In a business school, we pay the professors to teach. However, the students pay to learn as their MBAs will enhance their earnings in the private sector. In a School of Public Policy, we pay the professors to teach and we pay many of the students to learn. Many of the students are public servants from developing countries. Since a key mission of our School is to help improve governance and transform Asia, we will have to continue to provide scholarships to most of our students. This is why we will have to continue fund-raising despite our success.

Executive Education

We carried out our noble mission of educating the next generation of Asian leaders not just through our regular Master's and PhD programmes. We also did so through our Executive Education (EE) programmes. As Stavros documents in Chapter 2, we have been outstandingly successful in this regard.

We also believe that Executive Education programmes will remain a sunrise industry in our School. As the lives of public servants, especially senior public servants, become more hectic, it will be increasingly difficult for them to take a year or two out to do Master's programmes. Hence, we believe that we can fulfil our mission of training the next generation of Asian leaders on both tracks: the regular Master's programmes and the Executive Education track. The number of people who have gone through our Executive Education programmes is impressive: Altogether, we have had more than 8000 participants in these programmes.

What makes the success of our EE programmes even more remarkable is that our School adopted a "zero-subsidy" policy towards our EE programmes. Just as Mr. Lee Kuan Yew said that he would shut down SIA, a crown jewel of Singapore, if it stopped being profitable, we adopted the same policy at the LKY School: We said that we would shut down our EE programmes if they were not profitable. And, by following this clear and consistent policy, our EE programmes have proven to be profitable. And as Stavros shares in his chapter, our EE programmes have also helped our faculty significantly, in ways that go beyond the monetary aspect. They have provided us with the opportunity to interact with participants and to be exposed to public policies and practices already in place in other countries.

Challenges Peculiar to a School of Public Policy

Enough about successes. Let me now turn to the third part of my chapter: to discuss the constant challenges that any school of public policy faces, especially a new one like ours starting out in Asia (which has traditionally not had many schools of public policy). When I accepted the job of becoming the first Dean, I assumed that I was wading into a well-established industry. All that I had to do was to follow the advice of Dr. Goh Keng Swee, the former Deputy Prime Minister of Singapore. One of Dr. Goh's most memorable sayings which I have never forgotten is this: "Kishore, no matter what problems Singapore encounters, somebody somewhere has solved them. Go find the solutions and adapt them intelligently to Singapore."

A Non-Existent Gold Standard

When I became Dean in 2004, I assumed that my job would be an easy one. All that I had to do was to study and implement the best practices of public policy schools all over the world. By carefully and cleverly taking on board these best practices, I would help to propel the Lee Kuan Yew School of Public Policy into becoming one of the best in the world. It came as a big shock to me to discover after a few years that in the industry of public policy education, there was no readily available gold standard that I could hope to easily emulate and implement.

Why is there no gold standard? The simple answer is that public policy education is still not a "mature" industry and has not yet established global benchmarks and universally acknowledged standards of excellence. So the best way to tell this story is to compare it to the business school industry, which is one of the most mature industries in higher education. Nowadays, when someone graduates with an MBA, one can tell quite accurately what skills an MBA graduate has learned. There are some critical "core" skills that an MBA graduate is expected to have, such as finance and marketing. By contrast, when an employer interviews a graduate of a school of public policy with either a Master in Public Policy (MPP), a Master in Public Administration (MPA), or a Master in Public Management (MPM), the employer has no clear idea what knowledge or skills this graduate has acquired. Indeed, this failure of public policy schools to agree on a common certificate like the Master in Business Administration (MBA) is one key part of the problem. If one looks at the best schools of public policy in the world, their students graduate with degrees of different titles.

To understand this confusion, just look, for example, at the double-degree programmes we have signed with SIPA, the LSE and Sciences Po. It is clear that any student of ours who graduates from this double-degree programme would get a Master in Public Policy (MPP) from our School. However, his or her second degree from SIPA would be a Master of Public Administration (MPA); from LSE, it would be a Master in Public Administration (MPA) and from Sciences Po, it would be a Master of Public Affairs (MPA). Surely an employer who interviews any such double-degree student will be confused. It would be legitimate for him to ask: "So what did you learn in your public policy education?"

Any graduate from our School can give the following honest answer: "We learnt some economics, some politics and a few things on leadership and management." This triple combination was not an invention of the LKY School. Instead, as we inherited the curriculum from the Harvard Kennedy School, we also inherited the philosophy of the curriculum from HKS.

Professor Joseph Nye told me in Davos that the most difficult courses to teach were those on leadership and management. Indeed, I subsequently learned that the HKS faculty was sharply divided on the question of whether leadership and management could be taught. Professor Richard Zeckhauser, who formerly taught PM Lee at the HKS, told me boldly that leadership could not be taught. Yet it is also a fact that the leadership courses at the HKS, taught by two gifted professors, Ronald Heifetz and Dean Williams, are immensely popular. The HKS has a bidding system to allocate scarce access to popular courses. Each HKS student is given an endowment of points per academic year to use during the bidding process. Traditionally, they would allocate a certain number of points to "buy" their way into popular courses. However, no student can get into the course of Ronald Heifetz without offering to give up all his or her points for one course. If the "market test" is the real test of the value of a course, then it is clear that the most valuable courses at the HKS are those in leadership.

Here, as another significant aside, let me mention an open secret in the HKS: On the one hand, there is enormous controversy among both the HKS faculty and students about the real educational value of the leadership courses taught by Professor Ron Heifetz and Professor Dean Williams. On the other hand, the vast majority of the students who graduated from these courses are wildly enthusiastic about the courses. In June 2008, Ron Heifetz and Dean Williams were awarded Harvard Kennedy School's inaugural Most Influential Course Award for their course, "Exercising Leadership: Mobilising Group Resources". This award was based on a vote by five-year *alumni* for the course that has had "the most influence in their post-Kennedy School career."[8] Incidentally, both Dean Williams and one MPM student who has participated in his course have told me that my book *The New Asian Hemisphere* is required reading for Dean Williams' course. My book discusses the broader challenges of the Asian Century and provides the larger context for a course on leadership.

Let me also add here that the HKS has done a comprehensive survey of their *alumni* to assess what they found to be of value from their education at HKS. Their results were shared with our School. And the results were truly revealing. When the graduates were asked which courses they studied most at the HKS, they replied, "Economics." However, when the graduates were asked which courses they valued the most, they said, "Leadership and management." This is a brief oversimplification of a complex survey but it brings out well the inherent tensions in designing the curriculum of a school of public policy.

Over eight years, I have had several conversations with fellow deans of public policy schools all over the world. From these conversations, it has become clear that schools all over the world are struggling to find the right balance. Scott mentions in Chapter 3 that Professor Kanti Bajpai, Scott and I were asked to submit a paper to a conference organised by GPPN at the Bellagio Center in Italy, on the experience of the LKY School in designing the courses and curriculum. In our paper, we suggested that global policy as a field of study is distinct from its "feeder" disciplines of economics, political science and management studies: (i) in the degree to which it is concerned with government policy-making towards the common good both at the global and domestic levels; (ii) in its multi-disciplinary nature; and (iii) in its focus on training public servants.[9]

The Bellagio conference was, by any standards, a blue-chip conference involving distinguished participants from all over the world. Such a conference was as good a place as any to assess the global consensus on what the curriculum of a school of public policy should comprise of. And it was clear after the three-day conference

---

8   "CPL faculty receive inaugural Most Influential Course Award", Harvard Kennedy School, Center for Public Leadership, 24 June 2008. Available at http://64.151.79.128/?cat=48.

9   Please refer to Appendix A, "Global Public Policy as a Field of Study: A View from Asia", by Kanti Bajpai, Scott A. Fritzen and Kishore Mahbubani.

that no such global consensus exists. Instead, schools all over the world are struggling to find the right balance. At the same time, some new schools are trying some innovative experiments. The Blavatnik School of Government of Oxford University will be opening its doors to its first batch of students in September 2012. Most public policy schools recommend a two-year programme for younger cohorts. Blavatnik is trying to do it in one year. Time will tell whether Blavatnik will succeed.

All this global uncertainty about the core curriculum of public policy schools clearly means that the Lee Kuan Yew School has to forge its own way in the coming decades. It has no established global standard to fall back on. Given our awareness of these challenges, our School set up a high-level panel of academics to advise our School in 2012. They comprised a group of four academics, namely Professor Abhijit Vinayak Banerjee, Massachusetts Institute of Technology; Professor Geert Bouckaert, Katholieke Universiteit Leuven; Professor Stephen Walt, John F. Kennedy School of Government; and Associate Professor Michael Mintrom, University of Auckland. After visiting our School in January 2012, they sent us an excellent report which is now being discussed with our faculty and Governing Board. We hope that at the end of this process the LKY School will have one of the best and most innovative curricula of a school of public policy. If others eventually come to learn from us, we will have made a meaningful contribution.

Significantly, several new public policy schools that have been set up in Asia are already coming to learn from us. Kazakhstan has decided to set up a Graduate School of Public Policy. To help it get started, the Nazarbayev University has signed a multi-year agreement with the LKY School. Several of our faculty members have been flying to Kazakhstan to provide timely and relevant advice. In addition, the Jindal School of Government and Public Policy (JSGP) has been set up in Delhi. Two of their faculty members came to spend a week with us. When they returned, Professor C. Raj Kumar, the Vice-Chancellor of the O.P. Jindal Global University, wrote me a note to say: "I am writing to thank you profusely for facilitating a very intellectually stimulating visit to the LKY School of Public Policy. The one week spent by us at the LKY School of Public Policy was truly inspiring and we are confident that it will significantly contribute towards shaping our own efforts at the Jindal School of Government and Public Policy (JSGP). We saw firsthand the extraordinary commitment to institution building and excellence among faculty, students and staff at LKY that makes your School a unique and transformative initiative in Asia, which has far wider implications for the systematic study of public policy in all its dimensions. We sincerely hope that the LKY School will not just be our role model, but our institutional mentor in this endeavor."

Clearly, even though our School is still on a learning journey as we try to work out the best possible curriculum and academic content, we have already begun sharing the fruits of our learning journey with others.

The "Asian" Identity Question

The second constant challenge can be put in the form of a simple dilemma: Do we want to be the best School of Public Policy in Asia, or do we want to create an Asian School of Public Policy? If it is the former, we will try not to work out a distinctive Asian identity. Instead, we should implement the best academic practices worked out by leading public policy schools, all of which are Western now. Hence, we would have a more "Western" identity as a result. But if we make the latter choice, we will start from the assumption that given the different environment in Asia, we will have to develop a School of Public Policy that responds to the special needs and circumstances of our region.

A small concrete example may help to explain the difference a little better. One key goal of a school of public policy is to promote good governance and to promote it by developing good studies of good governance. In the West, a necessary and indispensable condition for good governance is democracy. Indeed as far as any Western society is concerned, good governance is not possible without democracy. China does not have democracy. Yet it has enjoyed reasonably good governance in recent decades because its government has managed the largest poverty reduction programme in human history and is well on the road to producing the world's largest middle class. Many governments around the world envy what China has achieved. This example makes it clear that in public policy studies, there can be contradictions between Western theories and Asian practices. So what should the correct response of a school like ours be? Should we develop Asian theories of public policy?

Developing new theories in academia is inherently difficult. There are many reasons for this. Such major intellectual breakthroughs come through rarely, if at all. Also, if we try to develop theories that "work" only in Asia, we would have to deal with a major conundrum created by Western social science. It works on the assumption that if social science reaches a finding based on an experience in, for example, Boston, the finding has universal applicability. And if it does not have universal applicability, it does not qualify as social *science*, which, by definition, has to be universal in applicability.

One of the privileges I have had as Dean is to have attended many interesting academic conferences. Often I happened to eavesdrop on significant conversations. One such significant conversation I heard took place at a Davos GULF meeting I mentioned earlier. It was between then Harvard President, Larry Summers, and the Yale President, Richard Levin. If I remember the conversation correctly, Professor Levin was lamenting the poor understanding of the rest of the world in America. Larry Summers smiled and replied, "Rick, you are not mentioning the dirty words 'Area Studies', are you?"

Larry Summers knew that he was touching on a sensitive point. Since Western social science was developed on the assumption that it had universal applicability, Western social scientists felt little urge to study other societies to see if their theories worked well in other societies. They just assumed that they did. Hence, one of the strangest phenomena of our contemporary era is that even though our world is getting smaller and smaller and more and more interdependent, and therefore we have to understand non-Western societies better, Western social science is still not very interested in doing so. Many lay readers will be puzzled by such a claim. Those who doubt my claim should look at the contents of leading Western social science journals. By far, the huge majority of them are written by Western social scientists on Western experiences. Few of them have made an effort to understand how their theories work in non-Western settings.

This bias towards the Western experience has also created a problem for faculty in Asian schools. Since they live in and write about Asian societies, their chances of getting published in leading Western journals are much less than those of Western scholars. However, to get "tenure" in a leading global university like the National

University of Singapore, they have to publish in leading journals, which are mainly Western journals. In short, Asian social scientists do not compete on a level playing field with Western social scientists.

Let me stress here that I am not the first Asian academic to make such an observation. Two of Singapore's leading social scientists are Professor Linda Lim, teaching at the University of Michigan, and Professor Pang Eng Fong, teaching at the Singapore Management University (SMU). They published an article in *The Straits Times* which said, "Faculty whose interest is inter-disciplinary and topical, or in place-specific or policy-oriented research, may have difficulty getting published in the top 'internationally-refereed' journals, thus defined. Research questions important in small and developing countries may not be of interest to the global discipline, and sufficient empirical data may not be available to enable the use of sophisticated testing methodologies."[10] Professor Amitav Acharya, a Visiting Professor at our School, made this point in a 2007 lecture at Oxford University: "In the field of international relations, there is now a growing recognition that what passes for theory has been, and continues to be, shaped mainly by the Western ideas, experiences, and practices. [...] Some of the fastest advances in the discipline are taking place in non-Western countries, especially China, India and even Indonesia. In China, for example, some 48 universities are now conferring bachelor degrees in international studies. Yet, IR theory remains stubbornly Western, incorporating relatively few insights and voices from the non-West."[11]

Let me also add here that our Asian colleagues in the natural science departments do not have the same problems, at least not in the current trend or in the same degree. If an Asian scholar were to make a new discovery in mathematics or physics, chemistry of biology, there is no doubt that it would have universal applicability. However, one interesting phenomenon is taking place in the field of medicine. Our colleagues in the NUS have discovered, for example, that some anti-cancer medicines require significantly different dosages in Asian compared with Caucasian

---

10 Linda Lim and Pang Eng Fong, "What it will take to evolve world-class universities here", *The Straits Times*, 14 July 2003.

11 Amitav Acharya, "International Relations Theory and Western Dominance: Reassessing the Foundations of International Order", Lecture delivered at the "Reenvisioning Global Justice/Global Order" Seminar Series, Centre for International Studies, Oxford University, 22 February 2007.

patients. It has also been shown that lung cancer, stroke, dementia and obesity are different diseases in Caucasians and Asians. Such findings have shown that we have to be cautious about assuming that Western medical science has universal applicability. Our challenge in the field of the social sciences is to see whether we can make similar findings in this field.

These challenges are enormous but we should not lament them. Instead we should welcome the opportunity to make contributions in the field of the social sciences on a scale similar to those already made by Western social science. Here, the LKY School has massive intellectual opportunities as it looks to the future. It can begin to provide alternative points of view. And I have no doubt that our Western academic colleagues will welcome this. They would welcome any additions to the body of knowledge that humanity has been accumulating.

To begin with, one small contribution that the School can make is to produce more Asian case studies. Public policy schools, like business schools, use many case studies in classroom teaching. Today, HKS has the largest bank of case studies. We use many of them in our classrooms. We know that the HKS faculty will be happy to see the LKY School produce more Asian case studies and indeed they proposed to help us do so.

Hence, in response to the question that I posed at the very beginning of this segment of my chapter, the answer of the LKY School is that we want to do both: We want to become the best School of Public Policy in Asia and also to create a new Asian School of Public Policy. It is our hope that our School will generate case studies and academic journal articles and other literature which both Asia and the world will find to be useful and relevant. Pushing the frontiers of knowledge is one of the noblest human endeavours. It is truly fortunate that the LKY School has the opportunity to do this in a significant way in the 21st Century.

The Market for Public Policy Education

The third constant challenge that our School faces, in common with other schools, is that the "market" for public policy education is surprisingly small. Stavros points out in Chapter 2 how McKinsey made this discovery when they looked at prospects for our School. The small size of the market becomes very clear when one looks at the number of applicants each year who apply to do an MBA at business schools, compared to those who apply to schools of public policy. Hence, as Dean of a school of public policy, I look with envy at my counterpart at the NUS Business School. Each year, he gets approximately 4,000 applicants for the MBA programme while we get 750 applicants on average for our MPP, MPA and MPM programmes every year.

Why do more young people prefer to study in business schools rather than public policy schools? Here again, there must be many reasons. The business school industry is a more mature industry than the public policy school industry. It may be only a matter of time before we catch up in size and volume. However, I am not optimistic that it will happen soon. The simplest reason why more young people prefer business schools to public policy schools is that a graduate of a good business school gets an immediate financial reward. As a *Forbes* article put it, "Graduates at the top business schools typically get their hefty investment back within four years of leaving school."[12] For example, graduates in Harvard's Class of 2006 saw their median salaries soar from USD79,000 before school to USD230,000 in 2010, which was the highest among US schools.[13] Indeed, I read constantly in the *Financial Times*, *The Economist* and other leading finance journals how business schools compete to show the dramatic salary increases that follow the attainment of an MBA.

To the best of my knowledge, no school of public policy anywhere claims that its graduates get a major increase in income after graduation. Indeed, it would be practically impossible to do this because most civil services in the world (with the possible exception of Singapore) pay relatively poorly. The Prime Minister of India, Dr. Manmohan Singh, has a basic salary of USD4,106 annually. Even with the inclusion of cash allowances, he earns only USD1,064 a month.[14] By contrast, a young MBA graduate from an Indian School of Business can easily hope to earn

---

12 Kurt Badenhausen, "The Best Business Schools: A Complete List", Forbes.com, 8 March 2011. Available at http://www.forbes.com/lists/2011/95/best-business-schools-11_land.html.

13 Kurt Badenhausen, "The Best Business Schools", Forbes.com, 8 March 2011. Available at http://www.forbes.com/sites/kurtbadenhausen/2011/08/03/the-best-business-schools/.

14 "A Raise for Prime Minister Manmohan Singh?", *The Wall Street Journal*, 23 July, 2010. Available at http://blogs.wsj.com/indiarealtime/2010/07/23/a-raise-for-prime-minister-mamohan-singh/.

USD120,000 annually if he joins McKinsey or Goldman Sachs. In short, it makes sense for ambitious young people who are in a hurry to improve their material livelihood to enrol in business schools.

Increasing the "market" for public policy education is a common challenge faced by public policy schools all over the world. There will be no easy short-term fixes. However, as more and more nations develop successfully, especially in Asia, the salary scales and working conditions of people working in the public sector, whether in government or in non-governmental organisations, will continue to improve slowly but steadily. This will in turn create a slowly rising tide of applicants to public policy schools.

One real blessing that the LKY School has in dealing with this constant challenge of a small "market" for public policy education is that we have been blessed with scholarships. Without these scholarships, it would have been difficult for the School to fulfil its core mission of improving governance in Asia. With these scholarships, public servants in Asian developing countries, including Cambodia and Laos, Myanmar and Bangladesh, are able to take time off their work to enrol in our Master's programmes. The founding fathers of the LKY School were truly far-sighted in recognising that without this generous pool of scholarships, the capacity of the School to grow would have been truly limited.

These three challenges of developing an excellent curriculum, the Asian content of our School and the small size of the pool of applicants to public policy schools will remain constant challenges. They will not go away soon. Like public policy schools all over the world, we will have to deal with these constant challenges.

Conclusion

Despite these challenges, as we look down the road and contemplate the future of the LKY School, there can be no doubt that a great future beckons. Why do I say this? The School was set up at the right time in the right region and in the right city. It was set up at the right time because governance is back. In the 1980s, 1990s and 2000s, the Western world was enthralled by the Reagan-Thatcher revolution. Ronald Reagan famously declared in 1981, "Government is not the solution to our problem; government is the problem." This attitude towards government in what was known as the Reagan-Thatcher revolution led inevitably to the devaluation of the public sector and the glorification of the private sector. Hence, in the Anglo-Saxon world, there developed a belief that if you were really smart, you would not go into the public sector. You would go and join a bank, a consulting firm, or a multinational company in the private sector. And, if you were young and idealistic, your inclination would be to join an NGO since NGOs were deemed in the West to be more "pure" than government agencies.

The 2008–2009 Western financial crisis was painful for the West. Equally importantly, it may have provided the Western countries with a painful reminder that governments are important. When the chips were down and banks began to fail all over the place, only governments could come in and rescue the global financial system. Surely the big lesson that the world should learn is that we have to constantly ensure that sufficient talent goes into governments to ensure that all societies get the best possible public goods. And if critical public goods like safety and security, education and health care, or even water, electricity and waste disposal are not provided well, the private sector cannot perform.

One of the key lessons we have learnt from the latest financial crisis is that public goods are essential to keep societies in good shape. The well-known *Financial Times* columnist Martin Wolf describes well the importance of public goods: "Public goods are the building blocks of civilisation. Economic stability is itself a public good. So are security, science, a clean environment, trust, honest administration and free speech. The list could be far longer. This matters, because it is hard to secure adequate supply. The more global the public goods the more difficult it is. Ironically, the better we have become at supplying private goods and so the richer we are, the more complex the public goods we need. Humanity's efforts to meet that challenge could prove to be the defining story of the century."[15]

In short, the 2008–2009 Western financial crisis has provided public policy schools an immense opportunity to demonstrate that they are providing a valuable public service. As a result of this, the public at large also needs to be educated about the importance of public policies. The time has come to launch a global political and

---

15 Martin Wolf, "The world's hunger for public goods", *Financial Times*, 24 January 2012. Available at http://www.ft.com/intl/cms/s/0/517e31c8-45bd-11e1-93f1-00144feabdc0.html.

intellectual revolution to boost support for public policy education. If this revolution succeeds, public policy schools all over the world will then have a more benign environment to operate in.

Given this global backdrop, we should not be surprised if public policy education begins to be viewed as a sunrise industry. New schools are sprouting up everywhere. Even Oxford University, as mentioned earlier in this chapter, has set up the Blavatnik School of Government. Many more are being set up in other regions of the world. Even though all these new schools will provide new competitors for the LKY School, it is also clear that it is better to be in a sunrise rather than a sunset industry. More schools will also create more possibilities for collaboration and help enlarge the market for public policy education for everyone. In keeping with the times, the Global Public Policy Network, which began with four schools, will increase to seven schools in 2012.

It also helps that the School has been set up in Asia. There is no doubt that the 21st Century will be the Asian century. Certainly, as the European and American economies keep limping along, growth rates in Asia will also slow down. China may grow at only 8 percent a year and India at 7 percent a year. Yet there is also no doubt that these are, by most historical standards, relatively high growth rates. The real big challenge for Asian societies is not just about sustaining their economic growth rates. It is also about developing new forms of governance to accommodate the needs and interests of the new middle classes that are emerging. Indeed, there will be a huge explosion in the number of middle class populations in Asia. In 2012, there are approximately 500 million people living in middle classes. By 2020, the number will explode to 1.75 billion people.

It would be unwise for Asian governments to continue on auto-pilot as their societies experience a major transformation. All the governments of Asia will have to adapt and adjust their methods and means of governance. Indeed, many have already begun doing so. It is also clear that many are learning from each other. In the midst of this great search for best methods of good governance in Asia, there will inevitably be a need for a great intellectual watering-hole to bring together current and future generations of Asian policy-makers to study and reflect on best practices. The LKY School is ideally placed to provide this service to the Asian region. We expect a surge in demand for both the regular educational programmes and the research projects of the LKY School.

Finally, we are truly blessed that we have been set up in Singapore. Singapore is by no means perfect. In May 2011, prior to the 2011 General Elections, PM Lee admitted, "No government is perfect . . . we will make mistakes. But when it happens we should acknowledge it, we should apologise, take responsibility, put things right."[16] The elections of 2011 showed that there has been some public dissatisfaction with some of the policies of the Singapore government. The Singapore government has publicly acknowledged that it will take on board some of these new public sentiments. In his August 2011 National Day Rally speech, PM Lee said, "My government will reach out to all segments of Singapore society to understand your perspectives, to share ideas and concerns with you, to work with you to come up with plans and programmes which will benefit all of us."[17] In April 2012, PM Lee even set up a Facebook page to collect feedback from and directly engage with the citizens of Singapore.

Yet, despite this increase in dissatisfaction, there is also no doubt that many of Singapore's public policies continue to enjoy the admiration of policy-makers all over the world. The well-known *Washington Post* columnist, Matt Miller, put it well when he said, "Singapore thus stands as the leading modern example of how development as pragmatic problem-solver can dramatically improve people's lives. This ethos has virtually disappeared from U.S. governance at the national level."[18] He added, "The island's real ideology is pragmatic problem-solving. It works thanks to cultural traditions that let this eclectic blend flourish. The system is nurtured by

---

16 Alicia Wong, "PM Lee: I'm sorry for our mistakes", Yahoo! News Singapore, 3 May 2011. Available at http://sg.news.yahoo.com/blogs/singaporescene/pm-lee-didn-t-m sorry-152850327.htm.

17 Prime Minister Lee Hsien Loong's National Day Rally 2011, 14 August 2011, at University Cultural Centre, National University of Singapore. Speech available at http://www.pmo.gov.sg/content/pmosite/mediacentre/speechesninterviews/primeminister/2011/August/Prime_Minister_Lee_Hsien_Loongs_National_Day_Rally_2011_Speech_in_English.html.

18 Matt Miller, "What Singapore can teach us", *The Washington Post*, 2 May, 2012. Available at http://www.washingtonpost.com/opinions/what-singapore-can-teach-us/2012/05/02/gIQAlQEGwT_story.html.

talented, highly paid officials who have the luxury of governing for the long-term without being buffeted much by politics."[19]

As the world as a whole struggles to find the best right mix of policies to cope with an increasingly complex policy-making environment, there is also no doubt that Singapore has already become a sort of Mecca for policy-makers globally. Indeed if one were to look all around the world for an ideal policy-making laboratory, it would be hard to find one that can match Singapore's experience. One of our former Visiting Professors, the development economist Dr. Henri Ghesquiere, says very insightfully that what distinguishes Singapore public policies from those of many other countries is how "integrated" they are. He says, "Singapore followed an integrated approach to development. Outcomes, policies, institutions, social and cultural values and the political dynamics of implementation reinforced one another."[20] Few other countries can match this record of governance.

This combination of being in a sunrise industry in a sunrise region and in a sunrise city provides a truly auspicious environment to grow the LKY School of Public Policy and to lift it to new heights in the coming decades. Success is not guaranteed. As investment managers wisely advise, "Past performance is no guarantee of future success." It would be absolutely foolish for the LKY School to become complacent. Yet it would be equally foolish for the LKY School to not take advantage of the brilliant new opportunities that are surfacing. As Shakespeare said in his usual brilliant manner, "There is a tide in the affairs of men/Which, taken at the flood, leads on to fortune."[21]

The tide has arrived. We can now sail forth.

---

19 Matt Miller, "What we can learn from Singapore's health-care model", *The Washington Post*, 3 March 2012. Available at http://www.washingtonpost.com/wp-dyn/content/article/2010/03/03/AR2010030301396_pf.html.

20 Henri Ghesquiere (2007), *Singapore's Success: Engineering Economic Growth* (Singapore: Thomson Learning), p. 167.

21 Julius Caesar Act 4, Scene 3, 218–219.

2 Building a World-Class School of Public Policy

Stavros N. Yiannouka

Mr. Lee Kuan Yew Meets McKinsey & Company

In early 2004 the partners at McKinsey & Company decided to hold their annual conference in Asia for the very first time. The location chosen was Shanghai. As was traditionally the case for events of this kind, McKinsey wanted a high-profile Asian leader to address the gathering. Not surprisingly, then Minister Mentor Lee Kuan Yew was quickly identified and invited to be the guest-of-honour. He accepted, on the condition that McKinsey & Company make a charitable donation to a cause of his choosing. In *lieu* of the donation, McKinsey offered to develop a strategic blueprint for a new graduate school of public policy in Singapore, named in honour of the Minister Mentor — an offer that was accepted. And so begun the somewhat improbable story that less than a year later would see me leaving McKinsey & Company to join the newly established Lee Kuan Yew School of Public Policy at the National University of Singapore.

The McKinsey Study

In September of 2004, I was appointed by McKinsey & Company to lead the project team that would develop the strategy for the newly created Lee Kuan Yew School of Public Policy at the National University of Singapore. Two partners, Jean-Marc Poullet, then head of McKinsey in Southeast Asia and Mayank Parekh, then head of the Singapore office, provided direction and oversight, as was the practice. The initial team on the ground comprised three young Singaporean consultants. Our mandate was to carry out work over two phases — first, to develop a strategy for the School and second, to propose a plan for implementing that strategy. For this task we were asked to work closely with Francis Chong, the School's Director (Strategic Planning) who was on secondment from the Singapore Administrative Service.

Size of a School: How Big is Big Enough?

As a problem-solving challenge the assignment — to develop a strategy and implementation plan for the School — appeared fairly straightforward. The School as we found it in 2004 was very small. It had 11 faculty members and 40-odd students across two Master's degrees inherited from the public policy programme of the National University of Singapore (NUS) Faculty of Arts and Social Sciences. For it to stand any chance of establishing itself as a regional, let alone a global, player, it had to grow significantly. The question was how big was going to be big enough? As we looked around the world of public policy schools we found that they came in many different shapes and sizes, from the gargantuan with over a thousand students (the Harvard Kennedy School and the School of International and Public Affairs at Columbia) to the boutique with fewer than two hundred (the Woodrow Wilson School at Princeton and the Goldman School at Berkeley). Moreover, the discipline was overwhelmingly centred in the United States. At the time there were no European schools of note other than France's fabled *École nationale d'administration* (ENA) and that appeared to be an altogether different proposition with a staff of a few hundred, of which only a handful were permanent teaching staff, serving the needs of some five hundred students.

Mayank Parekh finally broke the deadlock. He, together with Francis Chong, had travelled to the United States to conduct a series of face-to-face interviews with leading deans and academics at various policy schools. There they learnt that an academic discipline typically required a minimum of seven or eight faculty members to provide the critical mass of intellectual capital. As public policy education was founded on three disciplines — economics, politics and management — Mayank reasoned that the School would need around 20 to 25 (roughly 7 or 8 for each discipline) faculty members in order to be academically credible. As the higher education industry standard seemed to be for graduate schools to have a ratio of about ten students to every faculty member, this implied that the School should aim for a minimum enrolment of two hundred and fifty students. Borrowing (somewhat liberally) from industrial economics, the team termed this the minimum efficient scale that the School needed to achieve.

Sizing the Market for Public Policy Education in Asia

We then turned our attention to determining where these students were going to come from and what kind of an education was likely to appeal to them. We knew, of course, that the vision of the Singapore government in establishing the School was to help raise standards of governance in the region by providing a world-class education in public policy to regional policy-makers and public sector leaders. But why would these policy-makers and leaders choose, first, to study public policy, and second, to do so in Singapore at a new school without an established track record? Furthermore, although the mission of the School was oriented towards the region, it would nevertheless be important to demonstrate that it could attract a core of promising Singapore civil servants to its classrooms. Given that the civil service in Singapore was widely acknowledged to be the most advanced and professional in the region, we reasoned that the School needed to appeal to its demanding home market first before it could credibly seek to attract students from overseas.

Our early findings in this regard were not encouraging. Together with Jean-Marc Poullet, I interviewed all the permanent secretaries then heading the various ministries across Singapore. There we learnt that while many of them had benefitted from a public policy education (mostly obtained at the Harvard Kennedy School), this type of education was not necessarily popular with younger civil servants. Moreover, the civil service in Singapore was no longer prescribing the kind of degrees that it would support but was leaving the choice entirely to the individual civil servants. Many were increasingly opting for an MBA degree as a viable alternative that also offered career opportunities beyond the public sector.

To explore the motivations of students and glean from them the basic value proposition of an education in public policy and its related fields, we also surveyed and interviewed a cross-section of McKinsey consultants who had graduated from policy schools, including Chelsea Clinton, daughter of former President Bill Clinton and Secretary of State Hillary Clinton who had just graduated from Oxford with a Master of Philosophy in international affairs. Unfortunately our findings were again not particularly illuminating. It seemed that most policy graduates we talked to selected their degrees for fairly generic reasons; namely, to obtain a good general education and some useful skills, to network with peers who were "going places" and (perhaps most importantly) to improve their career prospects.

To conclude our analysis of the likely market, the team crunched some numbers to determine the likely demand for overseas graduate policy studies in Asia. We analysed publicly available data on inter- and intra-continental student flows across all disciplines and made some assumptions regarding the likely take-up rate for policy studies based on published data from graduate schools in the United States. Our findings were sobering. The likely market — Asian students who would be interested in pursuing a policy education in an Asian country other than their own — was going to be small, at best a couple of thousand each year but in reality, after adjusting for English language proficiency and other criteria of academic suitability, potentially far fewer. All of a sudden, the minimum efficient scale of two hundred and fifty seemed like a tall order. However, there was some consolation in the fact that we expected demand to grow in line with general economic growth in Asia and that aside from a handful of universities in Japan and Australia, there did not appear to be any natural competitors in the region. The School therefore was likely to enjoy something of a first-mover advantage.

Developing a Research Strategy

The final piece of the puzzle in the first phase of our work concerned the School's intellectual identity. What was the School going to be known for as a producer of knowledge? Consistent with our analysis that the School needed to attract Singaporean civil servants to be credible, the team also reasoned that the School's direct value to Singapore had to extend beyond educating a dozen or so civil servants each year. During our analysis of best-in-class policy schools (primarily in the United States) we noted that the best faculty at these schools often consulted on matters of policy with governments from around the world. Indeed many had periodically served in government and brought practical experience as well as academic rigour to their work. We coined the term "Singapore franchise" to denote the need for the School to become an active and relevant participant in the policy dialogue in Singapore. Of course the School could not hope to achieve this unless its faculty could produce research that was both timely and relevant. We therefore proposed that the School consider creating centres of research excellence and providing them with sufficient resources so that they could hire faculty and research fellows and develop clusters of expertise.

Beyond a general orientation towards Asia, we made no recommendations as to the research agenda that the School should develop. We recognised that this would in large part be opportunity driven and dependent on the interests of individual faculty. It was at this point of the project that we dealt with potentially the most controversial issue: the perception that there were limits to academic freedom in Singapore. This was a crucial matter. Public policy is by definition political and, as we had heard from both faculty at the School as well as those we interviewed overseas, there remained questions as to whether the environment in Singapore was sufficiently permissive to allow for dialogue between government and academia on potentially controversial issues of public policy. While it was not our place to proffer advice on this sensitive issue, we nevertheless decided to raise it as an area of concern, one that could hamper the future development of the School.

Meeting Minister Mentor

This first phase of the McKinsey study ended in November 2004, with Jean-Marc Poullet, Mayank Parekh and myself presenting our findings to then Minister Mentor (MM) Lee Kuan Yew at the Istana, in the presence of Kishore Mahbubani, Francis Chong, and Hsieh Tsun-yan, McKinsey's senior-most partner in Asia at the time.

MM Lee articulated his firm belief that it was in Singapore's own best interests to help in any way it could the countries in the region, particularly China, India and its partners in ASEAN, to raise their levels of governance. This was ultimately the mission he wanted the School to fulfil. A few days after our meeting with MM Lee, we were given the opportunity to present our findings to a Cabinet committee comprising then Deputy Prime Minister Tony Tan (currently President of Singapore), Minister of Defence Teo Chee Hean (currently Deputy Prime Minister) and Minister of Education Tharman Shanmugaratnam (currently Deputy Prime Minister and Finance Minister). The three Ministers reinforced the message given to us by the Minister Mentor and also assured us that the Singapore government understood what was required for a school of public policy to succeed and would be broadly supportive of the endeavour.

Joining the LKY School

I saw in the Lee Kuan Yew School an opportunity to contribute to creating an institution with a noble purpose. I met with Kishore and agreed to join the School as a Vice-Dean with responsibility for implementing the recommendations of the McKinsey report, to drive the growth and development of the School in line with the strategic blueprint that I had helped develop.

Student Recruitment

My first priority as Vice-Dean was to revamp the student recruitment strategy. The public policy programme had in previous years relied on advertisements to draw in applicants for its two graduate degree programmes: the one-year Master in Public Management and the eighteen-month Master in Public Policy. During the McKinsey study, the team had determined that advertising was not a cost-effective way of attracting the kinds of students that the LKY School wanted to recruit: namely in-service government officials or executives from the not-for-profit sector. Rather, we felt that the School should adopt a "wholesale" strategy and seek to recruit students indirectly by building relationships with the human resource departments of government organisations and agencies who would then help disseminate information about our programmes and either nominate officials or encourage them to apply directly to our School. Our principal value proposition to those agencies and indeed to prospective students was that the School could offer them a world-class education in public policy and public administration together with exposure to the public sector in Singapore, which was widely acknowledged to be a world leader in delivering good governance founded on well-reasoned public policies. We were also able to offer generous scholarship funding to some of the best students who might otherwise not be able to afford an overseas education.

It was for this reason that my team and I spent a considerable amount of our time in the second half of 2005 (as well as in the years that followed) travelling across Asia, going door-to-door promoting the School. Our priority countries were of course China, India and the member states of the Association of Southeast Asian Nations (ASEAN). But occasionally our travels would take us to more exotic destinations such as the Maldives. One of my earliest and most memorable trips took place in October 2005. The School had secured a commitment from the Villa Foundation to provide scholarships for studies at our School. The Villa Foundation was the charitable arm of the largest conglomerate in the Maldives. Its founder and chairman was Mr. Qasim Ibrahim, who was then also the country's Minister of Finance. And so it was that I visited the Maldives as a guest of Mr. Qasim. During the trip, we successfully concluded the negotiations for the award of scholarships for the School by the Villa Foundation and I participated in a televised signing ceremony at one of Mr. Qasim's resorts near the capital Malé.[1]

In 2005, the challenge of marketing the School was made all the more difficult by the decision to introduce a third degree programme, the one-year Master in Public Administration targeted at mid-career officials with a minimum of five years' work experience, and to transform the eighteen-month Master in Public Policy into a two-year degree programme targeted at younger professionals with one to three years of experience. Indeed for all effects and purposes the School had introduced two new degree programmes to replace the eighteen-month Master in Public Policy. There were a number of reasons that prompted the School to introduce these new degree programmes. Firstly, the management team felt there was insufficient differentiation between the two existing programmes, the Master in Public Policy and the Master in Public Management, as both were essentially targeted at the same potential students, namely mid-to-senior public sector officials from Asia. Secondly,

---

1   After the signing ceremony my wife and I sat with Mr. Qasim at the resort bar on the beach, listening to his amazing life story: how he rose from humble beginnings to become the Maldives' most successful businessman; why he decided to enter politics; and how he was imprisoned for his political activities only to be subsequently released and invited to join the government.

the one-year Master in Public Management that had been introduced only in 2001 could not support an intake of more than 25 students per year. This programme was fully funded by the Singapore Ministry of Foreign Affairs and included a costly half-semester component at the Harvard Kennedy School. Finally, the eighteen-month Master in Public Policy degree programme was something of an awkward construct that did not fit in with our emerging plans to expand our network of strategic partners, primarily through the establishment of double-degree programmes.

Notwithstanding the challenges we faced, the results of our first full-fledged student recruitment campaign exceeded our expectations. Whereas in the past the public policy programme had struggled to attract more than 150-odd applicants for the eighteen-month Master in Public Policy, the LKY School in its first full year of operations attracted over 400 applications for the two new degree programmes.

Strategic Alliances and Partnerships

The Harvard Kennedy School (HKS) was from the early days of the public policy programme in the 1990s the LKY School's most important strategic partner. Indeed the HKS played an important part in supporting the early development of the public policy programme of the National University of Singapore (NUS). Dr. John Thomas, a very tall and very affable faculty member, who was known by staff in Singapore as "Papa John", was Chair of the Singapore Programme at the Harvard Kennedy School. He had spent several years in Singapore in the mid-1990s and along with Dr. Ong Jin Hui and Dr. Teng Su Ching had built up the public policy programme within the NUS faculty of Arts and Social Sciences.

One of the first tasks assigned to me when I came on board in mid-2005 was to conduct a comprehensive review of the LKY School's relationship with the HKS. The report's conclusion was that "the relationship with the Harvard Kennedy School remained a potentially significant yet underleveraged asset for the Lee Kuan Yew School of Public Policy". This report was then redrafted into a letter, which Kishore sent to the newly appointed Dean of the Harvard Kennedy School, Professor David Ellwood, requesting that our two institutions work together in an effort to revitalise this important relationship. That led to two trips in quick succession to Cambridge, Massachusetts, where I held wide-ranging meetings with faculty and staff at the Harvard Kennedy School. I was very warmly received by all the people I met including David Ellwood, John Thomas and other old friends of the public policy programme such as Professor Tony Gomez Ibanez and Professor Kenneth Winston. It did not take me long to become thoroughly enamoured with Harvard and the quasi-bohemian environment of Cambridge. I also began to understand why Harvard was able to engender such loyalty amongst its *alumni*.

My personal sentiments, however, did not alter the report's conclusion that the fundamental structure of the relationship between the Harvard Kennedy School and the LKY School, which the latter inherited from the public policy programme, had been superseded by events. Specifically, the relationship was anchored in a contract for services whereby the HKS would periodically provide what can loosely be described as development assistance in building first a programme and then a school of public policy. While this assistance was necessary in the early years of the public policy programme, it was not clear why it remained so once the LKY School was up and running. The second pillar of the relationship was constructed around a memorandum of understanding whereby the HKS had helped launch the Master in Public Management degree, which incorporated a seven-week stint at the Kennedy School including a weeklong fieldtrip to Washington, DC. While the Harvard component was clearly a significant and very popular feature of the Master in Public Management programme, it too had been superseded by events. In particular, it was not clear why the LKY School, as part of a century-old university, should need to outsource the teaching of a part of its own degree programme. Let me add here that this conclusion could have been very different had the Master in Public Management been a joint or double degree. However, it was the policy of Harvard not to engage in double or joint degrees because it feared (quite legitimately) a dilution of its powerful brand.

In any event, notwithstanding the report's assessment, the School felt strongly that this relationship should be preserved and where possible strengthened. And so the strategic partnership between the LKY School and the Harvard Kennedy School persists to this day. There is no doubt that the School derives benefit from its association with the brand of the HKS. Moreover, the popularity of the Master in Public Management degree programme has been further enhanced by the extension of the Harvard component to a full semester. In addition, with the assistance of our "no-nonsense" Director of Finance, Domenica Piantedosi, we were able in 2010 to renegotiate and rationalise the agreements with the Harvard Kennedy School and place them on a more financially viable and sustainable footing. We have also been able to broaden the scope of the partnership to include jointly funded research seminars and workshops on topic areas such as Crisis Management.

Beyond the Harvard Kennedy School, our partnership strategy in the early years was very much focused on joining the Global Public Policy Network (GPPN). The GPPN was the brainchild of Professor Lisa Anderson and Dr. Robin Lewis who at the time were respectively the Dean and Associate Dean of the School of International and Public Affairs (SIPA) at Columbia University in New York City. Anderson and Lewis conceived of the GPPN as a broad yet tightly knit alliance of academic institutions, located in global cities and dedicated to advancing research, education and dialogue on policy issues of global concern. The other founding partners were Sciences Po, Paris and the London School of Economics and Political Science (LSE).

With Kishore's encouragement, I began to assiduously cultivate relations with these three institutions, starting with SIPA. In November 2005, after visiting Washington, DC to attend the Association of Public Policy Analysts and Managers (APPAM) and calling on the Harvard Kennedy School, I joined a group of faculty members — Mukul Asher, Scott Fritzen, Alex Mutebi and Suzaina Kadir — in New York for a two-day visit to SIPA. In addition to meeting with Lisa Anderson and Robin Lewis, we also met with a number of senior faculty and administrators including Professor Robert Lieberman and Dr. Rob Garris. To someone with a private sector background in corporate law and management consulting, these meetings seemed rather bemusing. Indeed they more accurately resembled an Edwardian courtship ritual rather than a commercial negotiation. SIPA (and subsequently the LSE and Sciences Po) played the role of the prospective spouse endowed with impeccable pedigree, whilst the LKY School was the *nouveau riche* suitor trying to advance through marriage into the upper classes of higher education.

Of our three prospective partners, SIPA proved the most amenable to having the LKY School as a full-fledged partner in the GPPN. Sciences Po, through its reformist President, Richard Descoings,[2] and its Vice-President for International Affairs, Francis Verillaud, also demonstrated a keen interest in partnering the LKY School.

In contrast, the intentions of the LSE were less easy to decipher. While the Director of the LSE then, Sir Howard Davies, and his then deputy, Professor Sara Worthington seemed eager to have us join the GPPN, there appeared to be some hesitation on the part of their faculty. When I visited London in 2006, Professor Patrick Dunleavy, then head of the Master in Public Affairs programme at the LSE, quizzed me on the state of academic freedom in Singapore. In answering the question I did not try to convince the LSE faculty that academic freedom in the social and political sciences in Singapore was as unencumbered as it was in London, Paris or New York. I did however argue that Singapore was gradually liberalising and that, as a consequence, there was and would be far greater academic freedom to critique policy in Singapore. Dunleavy seemed to be satisfied with my answer and gave the distinct impression that he was personally supportive of the LKY School joining the GPPN but that he was, in his questions, perhaps reflecting the concerns of a number of his more conservative faculty colleagues.

In any event, Dunleavy's questions on academic freedom in Singapore proved to be a very minor obstacle and by June 2007 the School was able to announce its formal membership of the GPPN and the launch of three double-degree programmes, one each with SIPA, LSE and Sciences Po, Paris. These double-degree programmes brought together the LKY School's Master in Public Policy together with the corresponding degree programmes for the other institutions. Each year a select number of LKY School students would be entitled to spend their second year at SIPA, the LSE or Sciences Po and in so doing graduate with two Master's degrees. A corresponding number of students from SIPA, LSE and Sciences Po would also spend their second year at the LKY School and graduate with a degree from it.

---

2   Richard Descoings was a remarkable individual in the context of French higher education. He drove the internationalisation of Sciences Po, Paris through the introduction of English language courses and degree programmes. By doing so he slaughtered one of the sacred cows of French higher education, namely the monopoly enjoyed by the French language in the country's *grandes écoles*. He also launched a series of community outreach programmes aimed at raising the enrolment of students from underprivileged backgrounds at Sciences Po, Paris. Sadly, in April 2012, Descoings was found dead in a New York City hotel room. He was only 53.

In October 2007, the LKY School hosted the annual GPPN Conference in Singapore. The School went all out to impress our new partners with our convening powers, lining up an impressive array of talent from the worlds of policy-making and academia including luminaries such as Anne-Marie Slaughter, who would later serve under Hillary Clinton as Director of Policy Planning at the US Department of State, and Mario Monti who today is the Prime Minister of Italy. The latter, in particular, made quite an impression. Mario Monti had recently retired from his post as the European Union's powerful Commissioner for Competition where he had broken new ground in the exercise of the European Union's authority. He had been responsible for blocking the merger between two US corporate giants, General Electric and Honeywell, the first time that a non-US Regulator had exercised such authority, and he had also imposed one of the largest ever fines — €500 million — on Microsoft for abuse of a dominant market position. Somewhat belying his reputation as a corporate giant-slayer, Mario Monti turned out to be a soft-spoken and unassuming gentleman, completely devoid of any of the "airs" that a number of individuals, many with far fewer accomplishments to their credit, tend to put on once they achieve a certain standing in life. In many respects, therefore, Mario Monti represents a model of the kind of highly competent but humble technocratic public servant that the LKY School hopes to produce from amongst its graduates.

The Conference we hosted represented something of a high point for the member group, in comparison with other conferences, in Beijing in 2008 and in London in 2010. This was in part due to an ongoing debate as to whether the GPPN should be a narrow group focused on deepening collaboration between its four members or whether it should be a broader-based network built around programmes and public policy schools. With the benefit of hindsight this tension was not surprising given the somewhat strange composition of the GPPN, which comprised two graduate schools of public policy and international affairs — the LKY School and SIPA — and two social sciences universities — Sciences Po and LSE. Matters were not helped by the departure of Professor Lisa Anderson from SIPA in 2008 to take on a new role as Provost of the American University in Cairo where she is currently the President.

In any event, the hiatus regarding the direction of the GPPN would continue until 2011 when the group achieved something of a breakthrough. Firstly the group agreed that there was a need to develop an institutional identity and the LKY School volunteered to draw up a charter, a kind of constitution for the GPPN that would clearly set out its vision and provide some organisational structures and processes to move things forward. Secondly, the group agreed that the GPPN should be built around graduate-level public policy educational institutions. This decision was reached in part because both Sciences Po and the LSE had moved to establish their own graduate schools or institutes of public policy. Finally, and perhaps most importantly, the group agreed on the need for controlled expansion to better reflect the global aspirations of the GPPN. This was a point on which we at the LKY School insisted on as a matter of principle. We argued that regardless of our elitist pretensions as a group, we could not hope to remain relevant for long if we became an exclusively North Atlantic grouping with a small outpost in Southeast Asia. Hence we insisted that the group expand to include at least one other institution from Asia and preferably also another from somewhere else outside Europe and North America. Indeed at one point we even took a leaf out of the history of the EU and threatened to block any future expansion unless it met our criteria of being globally diverse. Fortunately, earlier this year the GPPN finally agreed to invite three new members to join the existing four: Tokyo University's Graduate School of Public Policy, the Hertie School of Governance in Berlin and the Getulio Vargas Foundation in Brazil.

If the LKY School had its way, Peking University's School of Government would also have been invited to join the GPPN. Unfortunately, the political concerns of some of our partners militated against the invite at this point in time. We remain hopeful that this will prove to be only a temporary setback. It is not that we do not share some of our partners' concerns over limited academic freedom in China. However, we feel that academics oftentimes miss the wood for the trees when it comes to making decisions on points of principle. For example, if they were to look into Chinese history they might be interested to learn that Peking University has, since its establishment in 1898, been at the forefront of the development of political thought in China. So what is more likely to advance the cause of academic freedom in China — the exclusion of Peking University School of Government from the GPPN or its inclusion? Of course our good friend Professor Fu Jun, Executive

Dean of Peking University School of Government, would probably answer the question rather pithily with "neither" because he would argue that on the question of academic freedom as in many other matters, China will change at its own time and in its own way.

Regardless of any disagreements over the precise membership of the group, we firmly believe that the GPPN represents a unique opportunity to create a community of institutions dedicated to advancing research, education and dialogue on issues of global policy concern. Fostering the constant movement of faculty and students across borders to research, study and debate these issues can only be of benefit to the world at large.

Branding, Marketing and More Student Recruitment

Notwithstanding the broad existential questions regarding the future of the GPPN, the LKY School's acceptance into the global elite of public policy education was an almost instantaneous marketing success. From a branding perspective, the double degrees in particular proved very popular with current and prospective students because firstly they sent an important market signal that academic standards at the LKY School were equivalent to those of our GPPN partners; and secondly they provided students with an opportunity to have an educational experience in Asia without having to completely forgo an Ivy League, British or *grandes écoles* education. In its first academic year as a member of the GPPN, applications to the School increased by over 60 percent for the LKY School's core MPP and MPA graduate degree programmes.

Around October 2007, we brought on board a very dynamic woman, from India, Preeti Dawra — a graduate of Columbia University who had also, for a time, been a journalist with *Earth Times*. Preeti brought with her formidable skills in networking, particularly in India, where she seemed to be linked to almost every "who's who" in this vast country. Working closely together with Professor Shreekant Gupta a member of the LKY faculty, Preeti transformed the LKY School's image in India. Whereas in the past we had struggled to secure a sufficient number of promising applicants from India, by the time Preeti left the LKY School in early 2012, we had succeeded in not only getting an increasing number of Indian civil servants to apply for our degree programmes but also persuaded the Indian government to fund full scholarships to support a number of these civil servants. This remains a remarkable achievement and one that we hope to emulate with regard to other countries, for example, China.

The LKY School's prospects in the area of student recruitment were also helped by improved brand awareness. In 2007 and 2008 the School had undertaken a significant branding campaign orchestrated with the help of the world-renowned agency Ogilvy & Mather (O&M). Working with O&M, we produced a series of advertisements that we were all especially proud of. What we wanted to do with these advertisements was to break the mould of traditional advertising for educational institutions. Rather than pictures of shiny, happy people extolling the virtues of the "leadership" education they had obtained, we instructed O&M to take a leaf out of advertisements for *The Economist* and focus instead on intelligent wordplay built around some of the themes that we wanted the School to be associated with, for example, the rise of Asia; the aspiration of many young people to make a difference through their work; and the fact that the School was able to offer generous scholarships. O&M rose to the challenge and produced some very quotable print advertisements with taglines such as:

- *Discover the difference between* globalisation *and* global-is-asian;
- *Power is shifting to Asia. Are you?*;
- *Make a difference, while others are busy just making a career*; and
- *Education is expensive. Ignorance, more so. Which explains our generous scholarships.*

Over time the LKY School also experimented with online advertising, search engine advertising, and social media, and invested a considerable amount in revamping its website. However all of these efforts paled in comparison with the LKY School's most potent branding and marketing weapon: its founding Dean Kishore Mahbubani! No section on branding and marketing would be complete without acknowledging the significant impact that Kishore has had in branding and promoting the LKY School. Not only is Kishore a formidable networker but his various musings on the rise of Asia and the global shift of power from West to East have succeeded in capturing the imagination of both public intellectuals and the chattering classes at large. From the LKY School's point of view, Kishore's personal brand and network coalesced very nicely with Singapore's growth and emergence as a truly global city with impeccable governance credentials. This confluence of factors was instrumental in transforming almost overnight the LKY School into the speaking venue of choice for world leaders, academics and other opinion-makers. Tony Blair, Paul Kagame, Ma Ying-jeou, Li Yuanchao, Montek Singh Ahluwalia, Kofi Annan and Lech Walesa[3] are just some of the world leaders who have spoken at the LKY School in the past eight years. Indeed the LKY School acquired something of a reputation as an organiser of high-profile events.

The capabilities to organise events large and small were developed in 2006 when the LKY School was commissioned by Singapore's Ministry of Finance to organise a one-and-a-half day mini-Davos — the Raffles Forum — to coincide with the hosting in Singapore of the annual meetings of the World Bank and IMF. In order to help us execute this ambitious project, the School recruited Joval Pantangco who had just left McKinsey & Company and had previously worked with me on the study for the LKY School. It was Joval working closely together with retired Brigadier-General Tan Huck Ghim, the School's Director of Administration, and Francis Chong who put the Raffles Forum together, tapping on Kishore's network to bring together a very impressive array of panellists and speakers[4] for a discussion around the broad themes of good governance and globalisation. While the event was hailed as a success by participants and organisers alike, it did (with the benefit of hindsight of course) reveal the limitations of this kind of gatherings at producing any meaningful insights about even the nearest of futures. Although many of the

---

3   They are, respectively, the former Prime Minister of the United Kingdom, the President of Rwanda, the President of Taiwan, the Head of China's powerful Organisation Department and a member of the Politburo, the Deputy Chairman of the Planning Commission of India, the former Secretary-General of the United Nations and the former President of Poland and founder of the anti-communist solidarity movement.

4   These included Nobel Laureate Professor Amartya Sen, Professor Lawrence Summers, former US Secretary to the Treasury, Mr. Lee Kuan Yew, then Minister Mentor of Singapore, Suzanne Nora Jones, then Vice-Chairman of Goldman Sachs Group, Mr. Li Rongrong, then Chairman of China's powerful State-Owned Assets Supervision and Administration Commission, Mr. Martin Wolf, the Chief Economics Commentator of the *Financial Times* and many others.

speakers, panellists and participants represented major actors in or observers of global capital markets, very little was said that even alluded to the major financial crisis that would engulf the world just a couple of years later.

Ultimately of course, no amount of branding, marketing or high-profile event organising can substitute for the power that word-of-mouth can have in making or breaking the reputation of an academic institution amongst prospective students. The LKY School's *alumni* are therefore, far and away, its most important assets in terms of marketing. In this regard, the LKY School works hard to ensure that we actively engage *alumni* particularly in student recruitment. We do this not just through the usual email or newsletters but also by ensuring that on every student recruitment trip made by faculty and/or staff we organise an *alumni* social gathering. One of my most memorable gatherings of this nature took place in August 2011 in Thimpu, capital of the Himalayan Kingdom of Bhutan. I was there on a family holiday but had agreed to set aside a day for meetings and to host an *alumni* dinner. I had visited Bhutan the previous year together with my former employers McKinsey & Company to participate in a meeting with the Prime Minister of Bhutan. There was then a possibility that the LKY School might collaborate with McKinsey & Company to provide leadership training for top civil servants in Bhutan. What made the August 2011 *alumni* gathering so memorable was not only the fact that all but one of our 15 *alumni* turned up (the absentee was travelling overseas) but, more importantly, that some of our *alumni* had travelled, partly on foot, for almost half a day just to make it to the dinner. This was perhaps the most apt demonstration of the kind of loyalty that the LKY School was generating amongst its *alumni*.

Executive Education

Bhutan might, at first instance, appear an unlikely destination to travel to for promoting the School's Executive Education programmes. However by 2010, the LKY School's executive education business had grown so extensively that no place, at least in Asia, was too remote. Although the School's predecessor public policy programme had engaged in executive education training and had secured an important (and still ongoing) programme with Brunei Darussalam, the School's activities when I joined in 2005 were limited mostly to importing and marketing executive programmes from the Harvard Kennedy School.

Executive Education was built almost as an afterthought as it barely featured in the McKinsey study. But, as Vice-Dean and given that professional services was the only business that I really understood from the inside out, it occurred to me that executive education could be run like a professional service. My first decision was to mandate that the LKY School would break from the practice of the public policy programme and would no longer promote the executive programmes of other institutions. The second was that the LKY School would try to avoid launching many open-enrolment programmes but focus instead on customised programmes. In other words rather than putting together a programme and then trying to sell that programme to the unsuspecting public, why not approach organisations and work with them to design programmes that meet their specific needs? Borrowing liberally from my experience at McKinsey & Company, we introduced the concept of a pipeline to track potential executive education business from the receipt of an enquiry all the way to the delivery of an actual programme. We also created standard templates for pricing programmes, writing proposals and contracting Executive Education programmes. And we began to actively cross-sell the LKY School's executive education business alongside the degree programmes on our numerous overseas marketing trips. The third and final significant decision concerned pricing. Conventional wisdom would have us believe that the School, being a new entrant to this market, should price its programmes at or just below those of its main competitors. We decided to defy conventional wisdom and price our LKY School Executive Programmes at a significant premium from our competitors in Singapore and the broader region. We did this because we wanted both to signal the higher value of an LKY School education and to emphasise the need for our own faculty and staff to deliver a high quality of educational experience to justify the higher price tag.

Demand for the School's Executive Education programmes has grown exponentially from all corners of Asia. Whereas the degree programmes enrolled a few hundred students each year, executive education trained a few thousand, albeit on shorter, non-degree courses. Moreover, unlike the degree programmes where the LKY School was reliant on scholarships to entice students to enrol, we operated the executive education business on a commercial basis, able to turn a profit each year. Many of our faculty could earn (sometimes significant) additional income teaching on Executive Education programmes, but more importantly, they enjoyed the opportunity to interact and test their ideas directly with policy-makers from around the globe. Building a successful executive education business thus gave the School the opportunity to magnify its impact on policy-making in Asia.

Today, the LKY School's executive education business spans the entire continent of Asia. Our top three markets outside Singapore are China, India and the Central Asian Republic of Kazakhstan. The case of Kazakhstan is worth noting because it serves as a good example of why executive education is so popular with faculty. The LKY School's intensive involvement with Kazakhstan began in 2008 when I was invited to give one of the keynote addresses at a conference organised by the country's Academy of Public Administration and chaired by the President of the Republic, Mr. Nursultan Nazarbayev. In my address I shared at length my understanding of the basic principles of meritocracy and pragmatism that underpin the workings of the civil service in Singapore. President Nazarbayev then gave his own speech using the conference as a platform to announce far reaching and significant reforms to the civil service in Kazakhstan. Following that conference in Astana the LKY School began to be invited to organise a series of high-profile Executive Education programmes including one which we delivered last year for the Prime Minister and his Cabinet. It is not difficult to see why faculty enjoy interactions at this high level.

The LKY School is not only delivering high-profile Executive Education programmes to the country's leaders but we have also been engaged to support the development of a graduate school of public policy at the recently established Nazarbayev University in Astana.[5] It is worth noting here that an *alumna* of the School, Aigerim "Aika" Bolat, an ethnic Kazakh who was born and brought up in Mongolia, coordinates the School's work in Kazakhstan. Moreover the original

5   The other partners involved in supporting the development of undergraduate and graduate schools at Nazarbayev University include the University College London, Duke University's Fuqua School of Business, the University of Wisconsin-Madison, the University of Cambridge and the University of Pennsylvania, amongst others. Indeed the LKY School is the only non Anglo-American institution to have been engaged in this ambitious venture.

invitation to address the conference in Astana and to get involved in the setting up of a policy school there was orchestrated by another *alumnus*, Zhomart Abiyesov. This again demonstrates the growing importance of the LKY School *alumni* network.

Kazakhstan, of course, is not the only country where the School is having significant impact through executive education. In China, the School has, with the support of corporate donors such as Wilmar International, provided training to several hundred provincial officials. In India, with the support of Professor Shreekant Gupta, the School has grown its business and now regularly offers programmes to the Department of Personnel and Training, Indian Railways and the Office of the Comptroller and Auditor General. Closer to home, from 2007 to 2010, the School trained over a thousand Vietnamese government officials. The training programmes were designed to update the governance and public management skills of officials in view of Vietnam's accession to the WTO in 2006. And in Singapore itself the School, amongst others, regularly provides training to the Home Team and has recently launched a programme for local Not-for-Profit Managers in collaboration with the Tote Board.

As a commercial enterprise, success and failure in Executive Education are relatively easy to measure. In this regard, the School's Executive Education has been a major success. Moreover, the LKY School Executive Education team is potentially a microcosm of the kind of organisation that the School at large should aspire to create. The team is multicultural and includes both faculty and non-faculty who, for the most part, work very well together. It is non-hierarchical while respecting lines of responsibility and accountability. The team is entrepreneurial but does not in the process of innovation or fire-fighting jeopardise professionalism. And while it is performance-driven it is also collaborative and knows how to have fun.

Faculty, Management and Bureaucracy

Unlike most academic institutions, the LKY School was, at least in its early years, not run by its faculty. It was very much an enterprise driven by its top managers who would come together once a week as the Management Committee (MC) and make many of the key decisions. And what a motley crew we were. The original MC that I joined comprised the Vice-Dean (Academic Affairs), who at the time was

Associate Professor Hui Weng Tat; the Director of Administration, Dr. Tham Kah Poh, an experienced administrator who trained as a dentist; Dr. Francis Chong, a career civil servant; myself a former lawyer turned management consultant; and of course Kishore, a career diplomat. Dr. Tham would leave within a few months of my joining and would eventually be replaced by a retired Brigadier-General Tan Huck Ghim who had, amongst his many other distinctions, commanded the UN Peacekeeping Forces in East Timor. In other words, aside from Professor Hui (and his successors, Scott Fritzen and Darryl Jarvis), the rest of the MC members were not academics.

For most academic institutions, such a makeup would have been a recipe for disaster and would have completely delegitimised the MC in the eyes of the faculty. Not so in the case of the LKY School. Perhaps because the majority of us were not academics, we consciously tried to steer clear of interfering too directly with issues such as curriculum reform, or admissions, seen to be the exclusive purview of the faculty. Instead we focused on those areas where our diverse skill sets could add value. A good example of this was the acquisition by the LKY School between 2007 and 2009 of a long lease of the housing estate at College Green opposite the School's new home at the historic Bukit Timah Campus.

College Green, formerly the Dunearn Road Hostels, was built and used to house students of the University of Malaya and subsequently the University of Singapore in the 1950s and 1960s. However, in more recent times, it was leased out by the government for private housing. The estate was very popular because of its prime location and relatively low rental. I do not recall exactly when we became aware that the leases to the estate were due to expire, but once we learnt of that we became convinced it would be in the best interest of the School to acquire the lease of the estate. Up until that point, the LKY School had leased apartments in residential condominiums to house its overseas students. This was a cumbersome arrangement, as the LKY School had to negotiate with a number of different landlords and had little or no control over the rents being charged. As many of our students were funded by scholarships from the School's endowment and operating budget, this affected our bottom line. We prepared an analysis showing how the LKY School would over time be financially better off were it to acquire a long-term lease of the College Green estate. Persuaded by the findings, the whole Management Committee sprung into action. We made our case to the relevant government agencies and worked on developing the actual acquisition of and renovation plan for the estate. As a result by 2009 the LKY School took posses-sion of a beautiful, residential estate capable of housing over 200 students all within walking distance of its campus. Not only did this benefit the School financially, it also significantly enhanced its value proposition to students because henceforth we could offer them a truly residential campus experience — something we could not do before.

Of course it was not all plain sailing between faculty and management. In particular when it came to establishing the LKY School's centres of research excel-lence, we as management were too hasty in taking on what we perceived to be promising opportunities brought to us by external stakeholders — Singapore gov-ernment agencies, the Asia Development Bank, and others. We further compounded our error by appointing faculty recruited from outside the NUS to lead these centres. While individually quite accomplished, these appointments were disadvantaged in that they had few professional networks within the LKY School, let alone the NUS. As a result, many of the research centres became quite isolated and divorced from activities of the rest of the LKY School.

That is why in 2009 and 2010 the Management Committee undertook the painful restructuring of the LKY School's research centres of excellence in an effort to integrate them more tightly with the rest of the School. The trigger for the reorganisation was the departure of Professor Viktor Mayer-Schönberger whom the LKY School had two years earlier recruited from the Harvard Kennedy School. In order to attract Mayer-Schönberger to the LKY School we had agreed to fund the creation of a new centre of research excellence — the Information & Innovation Policy Research Centre — which he would lead. Mayer-Schönberger was a former software entrepreneur and an accomplished scholar in his early 40s. He had little trouble securing tenure at NUS before making his move from the Harvard Kennedy School. His areas of research interest on public policy and the internet were very much at the cutting edge of thinking in this field. His book *Delete: The Virtues of*

Forgetting in the Digital Age[6] published shortly after he joined the LKY School has become something of a reference text and is very much influencing the debate on internet privacy and data protection regulation in the European Union. Unfortunately in 2010, just two years after joining the LKY School, he was offered a position at Oxford University where he is now Professor of Internet Governance and Regulation at the Oxford Internet Institute. Aside from the obvious allure of a professorship at one of the world's oldest and most revered universities, Mayer-Schönberger left the LKY School in part, as he shared with me, because he had been unable to identify a community of scholars with whom he could interact with around his particular research interests. In this way we, management, learnt the hard way that academic research cannot easily be engineered but can only be encouraged to percolate from within the faculty. Moreover we also learnt that contrary to the mythology of academia, academic research is (and perhaps never was) a solitary activity but requires a community of scholars interacting, exchanging ideas and sometimes collaborating around overlapping but not necessarily coinciding research interests.

Occasional divergences between management and faculty were not the only tensions that the LKY School faced. Entrepreneurs and business people would not be surprised to learn that the School also faced some tensions with the bureaucracy of the NUS. As managers of a start-up, we had little patience in the early days with the often-cumbersome bureaucratic processes that had evolved over the course of the 100-year history of the NUS. These processes were designed primarily to control a very large, decentralised organisation operating in a fairly predictable environment. Clearly they were ill suited to the needs of a rapidly growing start-up operating in an unpredictable environment. This was particularly the case with respect to the human resource processes that were in place to manage the recruitment of faculty and staff. As a young and rapidly growing institution the LKY School was keen to bring new, highly qualified people on board quickly and was also prepared to pay a premium to do so. This was of course met with some resistance from the University's central administration who were concerned with what they perceived to be our somewhat

---

6   Published by Princeton University Press, 2009.

laissez-faire attitude to recruitment and compensation and believed that it was just storing up trouble for the future.

It turns out that both the NUS and we were right! There is no doubt that had the LKY School adhered each and every time to the letter of relevant NUS guidelines we would not have been able to grow at the pace and in the manner that we did. At the same time, the NUS central administration was right in predicting that our approach to recruitment would be problematic further down the line. And so it was that in 2008 and 2009 in the midst of the global financial crisis, we found ourselves as a management team having to work hard to rationalise the recruitment decisions we had made in previous years with respect to compensation and job titles. Compensation packages are, unfortunately, not as confidential as we would expect, in that both faculty and staff sometimes engage in benchmarking, hence all the more the need for a rational, defensible and easily explainable system. A similar logic applied to performance management and promotion. Whereas in the early years the School was very happy to take a valued employee and in one fell swoop promote him or her three or four ranks from Executive to Senior Manager, we soon realised that as we grew we could no longer do that without adequate systems and processes in place to ensure that the morale of the rest of the organisation would not be negatively impacted.

Lessons Learnt about the Academic Enterprise

Building an academic institution is far more complicated than it appears at first sight. Perhaps more than any other enterprise, an academic institution is far more dependent for its success on the quality of the human capital that it employs. Skeptics will, of course, argue that this is becoming increasingly true of most enterprises, particularly in the so-called knowledge economy. But this is only partly true. In most enterprises the corporate identity clearly trumps the identity of the individuals working for that institution. Moreover, the professionals working in these enterprises owe their primary allegiance to the entity that pays their salaries. This is natural. In academic institutions, however, this is not necessarily the case, particularly when it comes to academics. Most faculty members view themselves as independent professionals whose purpose is to utilise the scientific method in pursuit of an objective truth. Their primary allegiance is therefore owed to science and true scientists are supposed to transcend the institutions that employ them. Of course academia does produce great global brands; think of Harvard and Yale, Oxford and Cambridge. However in reality, these brands took a very, very long time to establish and represent but a tiny sliver of the world's myriad colleges and universities. In this context, it is more often the case that an academic institution will derive its reputation for excellence from the quality of the academics it employs rather than from any intrinsic brand value. This is almost certainly the case, for example, with the University of Chicago (established in 1890), which despite its relative youth has over the past century or so been the academic home to a disproportionate number of Nobel laureates.

The above are important principles to appreciate because they often lie at the heart of many of the tensions between faculty and management that persist in academic institutions. Oftentimes these tensions have more to do with perception rather than reality but they are nevertheless significant in so far as they explain the reluctance of faculty members to subject themselves to any kind of collective, corporate identity. Conversely, in the case of the academic enterprise itself, these tensions mean that there are very real constraints on the impact that branding and marketing can have in driving the growth of an academic institution. In other words, however good the branding and marketing of an academic institution might be, reality will inevitably catch up and it will be judged primarily on the quality of its academic staff and their performance as teachers and researchers.[7]

The above assessment also explains why word-of-mouth is far-and-away the most effective marketing and branding channel for an academic institution. Unfortunately it is very difficult to control and influence. For a professional

---

7   In this regard, the role of an academic administrator or manager is not too dissimilar to that of a man-
     ager or head coach of a football team. Although you have some flexibility to acquire new players,
     most of your team members would have been inherited from your predecessor. Some of your players
     are young and some are past their prime. Some are stars but many are not. Some like each other and
     get along while others pursue petty little vendettas. At least on paper, you have some influence over
     how your players deploy as a team and what tactics they might adopt given the likely opposition.
     Before and after the game and during the half-time break, you can encourage, cajole, threaten, bribe
     and even punish but when the whistle blows and the ball is in play all that you can really do is stand
     on the sidelines and watch. And the best that you can hope to achieve, if things are not going well for
     you, is that you might be able to bring on a super-sub to rescue the game.

school of public policy like the LKY School there are three sets of opinions that matter.

The first set of opinions that matter for an academic institution is that of its peer institutions and their faculty. As noted above, academics view themselves as independent professionals. The opinions of their peers therefore matter a great deal as they ultimately determine their standing within their chosen field of enquiry. And however much non-academics might complain about the arcane and self-indulgent nature of much of the research that is carried out in universities, it is important to recognise that things are unlikely to change so long as peer recognition remains the ultimate benchmark for an academic.

The second set of opinions and the one that arguably counts the most is that of past and present students who have had firsthand experience of the institution. That opinion is shaped by the quality of what is known as the classroom experience: namely, how good are the teachers, how challenging is the curriculum and increasingly, how good are the other students in the classroom. The opinion of students in a professional school however is ultimately shaped by what happens to them after they leave the classroom and try to enter or re-enter the workforce. Facilitating the career development of students is therefore of paramount importance for a school like the LKY School.

This brings us to the third and final set of opinions that influence the branding of a professional school of public policy, namely the opinions of the current and prospective employers of its graduates. If the role of a professional school is to prepare students to enter a given profession then its success or failure will ultimately depend on the extent to which its graduates are entering and succeeding in that profession. In this regard, schools of public policy like the LKY School are disadvantaged relative to other professional schools such as medical, law and even business schools. This is because unlike these other schools, there is no well-defined public policy profession.

It used to be the case at the turn of the 20th Century that public administration was a fairly well understood discipline that prepared graduates for careers in public service. Now there are many — amongst them Paul Volcker, former Chairman of the Federal Reserve in the US, who serves on the Governing Board of the LKY

School — who advocate that such schools should return to the unglamorous but very necessary business of preparing graduates for careers in public service. And to a certain extent this is what the LKY School is trying to do with its Master in Public Administration degree programme where we are trying to improve the skill set of those already in public service. This however is no longer sufficient particularly because, outside of the United States, the role of preparing graduates for public service resides not with universities and schools of public administration but with government-controlled civil service colleges and academies of public administration that often take a whole-of-career "cradle-to-grave" approach to the training of public servants. There is of course room for schools such as the LKY School to insert themselves in this process, as an increasing number of public services around the world offer post-graduate opportunities to their officials. However, as the experience of Singapore has shown, schools of public policy and administration are only one of any number of potential destinations of study for public servants. Indeed as noted earlier in the discussion of the McKinsey report, many are increasingly opting for business education as an alternative.

Another reason why focusing on public administration may no longer be sufficient is because the world of public policy and public administration is changing fairly fundamentally both as a result of globalisation and by the rise of the so-called third sector. The business of government, like commerce, is becoming increasingly global. As a result large swathes of policy-making are now taking place in regional and global multilateral settings. This growing interdependency between countries necessitates a new class of public servants who are able to operate in global settings, that is, able to go head-to-head with the very best of their peers from across the world. Developing in parallel with the globalisation of the business of government is the growing importance of the not-for-profit sector. This so-called "third sector" is exceedingly diverse and is undergoing its own very profound changes. The emergence of mega-foundations such as the Bill & Melinda Gates Foundation[8] with assets in the tens of billions of dollars and the work of social entrepreneurs such as Muhammad Yunus of Grameen Bank (another visitor to the

---

8   Bill & Melinda Gates Foundation and the Bill & Melinda Gates Foundation Trust.

LKY School) are transforming this sector into a real force for poverty alleviation, education, combating disease and ultimately economic development. All of these domains are no longer as previously monopolised by governments and a handful of government-linked development agencies and multilateral institutions. Not only is the business of government globalising, it is also to a certain extent being privatised by individuals.

Implications for the Future of the LKY School

The analysis above points towards a number of implications for the future of the LKY School. Firstly, both the globalising and simultaneous privatising of the business of government presents a real opportunity for the LKY School to focus its efforts on preparing its graduates for careers that focus on economic and social development either as globally oriented technocrats (something that Singapore as a whole is particularly adept at doing) or as management professionals and social entrepreneurs for the third sector. This is not to argue that traditional public administration does not remain vitally important to the future development of Asia and the world as a whole. Rather, it is to make the case that there are limits to the impact that the LKY School can have in influencing public administration in Asia through its graduate degree programmes. Even if all of our 400-odd (average annual enrolment) graduate students were public sector officials (which they are not), they would represent but a drop in the ocean, that is, the public sector in Asia. Better then to focus our efforts on training a more targeted group of globally oriented public servants and/or public-spirited young individuals who want to make their careers in the not-for-profit third sector. This should be the focus of the School's graduate education. Again this is not to argue that the LKY School should abandon traditional public administration programmes entirely. The School already provides a great deal of public administration and management training to a very significant number of public servants each year, through its Executive Education programmes. These programmes ought to be recognised as core to the mission of the LKY School to raise levels of governance across the region.

Reorienting the School's graduate degree programmes in the manner described earlier would, of course, require some fairly fundamental changes to the curriculum of these programmes. Beyond the formal curriculum, there is also a need to make significant investments in the professional development of LKY School students to ensure that they are truly marketable.

The success of a professional school of public policy will ultimately be judged by the extent to which its degree programmes contribute to the gainful and meaningful employment of its graduates. The imperative for graduates of the LKY School to find employment that is both gainful and meaningful is of critical importance. The LKY School should therefore be judged not solely on the basis of the quantum of job opportunities that it generates for its graduates. In this context, the LKY School should avoid the temptation of becoming, in terms of student career development, a slightly more public-spirited version of a typical business school, with the bulk of its graduates taking jobs in banking and consulting. While it will always be the case that a number of graduates will seek and find employment with such organisations, the LKY School should be explicit in communicating with students that its foremost objective is to prepare them for careers with a public-service orientation. By the same token, however, the School should be as expansive as possible in its definition of what constitutes a career with a public-service orientation. And this definition should almost certainly include multilateral organisations, social enterprise and the broader not-for-profit sector. While the LKY School is very well equipped in terms of preparing students for multilateral organisations, it will need to invest resources to develop the capabilities to prepare students for careers as not-for-profit professionals and social entrepreneurs.

Investing in the professional development of students (as well as in enhanced *alumni* services) will ultimately benefit the School in terms of its reputation amongst students and their prospective employers. In this regard it will yield qualitatively better returns than any expenditure on advertising or high-profile speaker events and conferences aimed at raising brand awareness.

The final implication for the future of the LKY School relates back to the earlier discussion on the nature of the academic enterprise and to some of the peculiarities of the academic profession. The School needs to significantly boost the research productivity of its faculty in order to ensure that they will receive recognition from their academic peers around the world. For this, the School needs to tackle head-on many of the School's non-academic stakeholders who may view research as an esoteric and ultimately futile exercise. Of course it is true that public policy, like business studies and indeed many of the other social sciences, does not lend itself to neat theoretical constructs and the search for an absolute truth in quite the same way that the physical sciences do. However, just because something is impractical (or even seemingly impossible) does not mean that it is not a worthwhile pursuit. At the same time, faculty at schools of public policy need to appreciate that they have chosen to pursue their careers in institutions that have been designed to support a particular profession, even one as poorly defined as public policy. They therefore need to ensure that whilst earning the respect of their academic peers around the world, their research and teaching must also remain relevant for practitioners of public policy.

* * *

As discussed in the introduction the search for better forms of governance and better ways to organise society is a pursuit that has concerned learned men from the time of Confucius and Socrates. It is an inherently noble endeavour. The LKY School has been given the opportunity and has the resources to make a meaningful contribution to this noble endeavour. Over the course of its first eight years, the School has succeeded in putting down firm roots and establishing itself as a significant new player in the world of graduate public policy education. The School has promise and potential. The next eight years will determine whether this promise is fulfilled and its potential fully realised.[9]

---

9   It has not been possible for me to acknowledge all of the many colleagues who have helped me and the other authors to bring the LKY School to where it is today. I do however want to make special mention of Hazel Tan who played a key role in driving the LKY School's early efforts at student recruitment as well as Teresa Mok and Denni Cawley (nee Jayme) who supported me in building our executive education business. Finally, I want to acknowledge the invaluable support given to me by my executive assistant Noraini "Nora" Kiemien who joined me from McKinsey & Company in 2009.

3 The Three Enigmas of Professional Policy Education

Scott A. Fritzen

The Setting: The Harvard Kennedy School, May 1999

". . . So it strikes me that the question is 'Are we trying to build a first-rate public policy programme that happens to be in Asia, or an Asian programme in public policy?'"

It was one of those times when one almost watches oneself say something — let's call it an academic out-of-body experience. The occasion was a faculty retreat with Harvard's Kennedy School of Government as the venue and facilitator, and around the table sat my future colleagues — some six current and future faculty of the NUS Public Policy Programme (one of whom, like me, had a newly minted job offer in his pocket and was joining the programme in some months). And as there was a momentary silence in the room, I wasn't sure if it was one of the more profound things I had ever said, or one of the least.

The question has yet to be answered conclusively; and my perplexity on the wisdom of even asking it still remains. And that's the nub of this chapter.

Professional policy education *per se* is an enigma — and not only in Singapore. There are many requirements of a first-rate school of public policy. Students and executive education trainees who are positioned to make a difference in the world must be recruited. They must benefit from an evolving curriculum that can enhance their judgement and professional acumen in a dynamic world, taught by faculty energised by their mission. And the School must itself engage with the evolving practice of global policy-making and policy education. As easy as it is to state these requirements, no one has figured out definitively how to execute these challenges well, at least not in a generic way that holds for the varied contexts in which policy schools are cropping up around the world.

For institutions like the LKY School, the challenge of solving the enigma — of figuring out what it takes to have an impact on the world as a policy school — is a real and ongoing one. This chapter documents some of our experiences trying to innovate in answering important questions — questions that define what it means to be a global *and* Asian policy school.

The Enigma of What to Teach

Even before the first students are recruited — and remarkably, even before even the first faculty take up their positions — comes the issue of curriculum design, of what to teach. This sounds as if it should be easy, but it has certainly proven to be a challenge, in this and in any other policy school that has been open to self-examination over the past few decades. The structural process by which our current curriculum came together falls into three phases, the first stretching back to before the School was founded, to its predecessor "Public Policy Programme" of the NUS Faculty of Arts and Social Sciences.

Laying the Tracks of the Curriculum

In the first, roughly from the founding of the Public Policy Programme (PPP) to the late 1990s, the policy curriculum at the National University of Singapore (NUS) by and large was designed to be a "no-frills" version of the Kennedy School of Government's Master in Public Policy degree. Capitalising on the partnership that the PPP enjoyed with Harvard, several Kennedy School faculty spent significant time in Singapore, providing advice and actually delivering core courses, such as *Political and Organisational Analysis*, for the MPP degree.

The second phase of curriculum development took off once it became clear that the Policy Programme was headed in the direction of becoming a School of Public Policy. In 2004–05, the programme had hired a critical mass of some eight faculty members, several of whom were newly minted PhDs. Remarkably, some remain with the School and play key roles to this day, such as Caroline Brassard (now Assistant Dean for Academic Affairs); M. Ramesh (currently one of the School's only tenured full professors); and Wu Xun and myself (both now tenured associate professors). These and a few other faculty formed a curriculum review committee under the able leadership of Associate Professor Hui Weng Tat, who brought a decade of experience in academic administration as well as a kind, soft-spoken, thoughtful temperament to this and many other tasks over his four years as founding Vice-Dean for Academic Affairs of the School. The committee spent literally hundreds of hours of collective time re-designing the programme's two degree programmes — the Master in Public Policy and its specialisations, along with the Master in Public Management — and (later) its Master in Public Administration and PhD degree programmes. Together, this group effectively laid the tracks for the curriculum.

I recall the process as being collegial and thoughtful, but truth be told, it was also quietly upsetting for some. Some of the main questions revolved around whether the team was getting the balance of mandatory courses — in economics, management, statistics, politics and so forth — right. Where did this balance fit among the other policy programmes — thousands of kilometres away — against which we bench-marked ourselves informally? Of course, the faculty who would themselves be delivering the new curriculum were precisely the main conspirators sitting around the table in the re-think. It would be comically over-the-top to invoke here the lofty Latin *quis custodiet ipsos custodes* (Who, then, guards the guardians?). But in the back-ground of such discussions, here as in similar institutions, lurks the silent question for faculty members: *How will this re-design affect "my" course in the curriculum? Will I be scripted out of the curriculum and* (cue fingernails-on-blackboard horror-film soundtrack here) *out of a job*?

Far-fetched? I do recall a more senior faculty colleague who missed a crucial curriculum committee meeting around this time, only to discover some weeks later that two courses that he taught had indeed been dropped from the "core" curriculum — the part which all students must take. He ended up resigning some months later. (For other reasons, I'm sure.) The point is: The old saw attributed to Kissinger (but more likely the brainchild of Woodrow Wilson), that *academic politics are so vicious because the stakes are so small*, should clearly be appended here for clarity. The stakes are small *for non-academic observers.*

The third and current phase of curriculum development corresponded with the consolidation of the School's heady growth. Fundamentally, the School's pro-grammes are sound and appropriately benchmarked against top-notch schools of policy and public affairs around the world; a number of external reviews of the School have confirmed this in recent years. Yet because of the amorphous and unsettled — *enigmatic* — nature of policy education, the School continues to grapple with three sets of tensions. (In part because curriculum debates can have a Nietzschean "eternal recurrence of the same" quality to them, these tensions can *feel* like a form of academic multiple personality disorder.)

Why is Introduction to Public Policy the Hardest Course to Teach in the School?

The first tension is that while public policy is unequivocally a respectable academic discipline (as anyone with a PhD in the field will insist) — centred on the study of the policy-making process, it is also seen (notably by everyone else) as a multi-disciplinary free-for-all: the academic world's World Wrestling Federation. Rather than a coherent academic discipline with its own distinctive pedigree,[1] it becomes in this view an arena into which "gladiators" could enter in order to address and propose solutions to public problems, from an armchair or otherwise. To do so, one would draw liberally on the fruits of both "real" disciplines (such as political science and economics) and other "softer" quasi-disciplines (such as management or leadership studies). As one of our faculty members, the distinguished economist T.N. Srinivasan of Yale (and Yong Pung How Professor of our School) shared in a recent faculty meeting, throwing up his arms in mock confusion, "When I came here I had to figure out what this thing called public policy was." He quipped in his inimitable voice — so soft everyone in the room would strain to hear, "and I

---

1   Economics sports Adam Smith and Karl Marx. Political Science has Machiavelli and Woodrow Wilson. Public Policy's founding father is the considerably less well-known Harold Lasswell, a mid-20th Century American political scientist himself.

still — don't — know." (This, despite the fact that he has produced seminal works on, among other topics, India's economic reforms!)

The question of how to define and teach the core of the discipline is never settled; a curriculum review of any of the constituent degree programmes is never more than one anxiety-producing question away, kept at bay perhaps only by the sheer fatigue such reviews can inspire. On one level, the question boils down to alchemy, to how we ensure that the three primary building blocks of public policy — political science, economics and management — co-mingle in the right quantities in the core curriculum, while still leaving room for a good number of elective courses and for specialisations. On another and more important level, though, it becomes the question of how one conceptualises the field as a whole, as an entity that is greater than the sum of its parts.[2]

The "Introduction to Public Policy" course in the MPP degree would be a logical place to look for the faculty's collective answer to that question. Yet the paradox is that in a policy school, it is none other than this course that has proved the hardest to teach well, at least as suggested by the results of student feedback exercises. In these exercises, students confidentially submit to the central administration their assessment of a course and the quality of the instructor's teaching, using both numerical scores and open-ended comments. At the LKY School, we have had an array of faculty — some junior and some senior, including at least four who have written international textbooks on the subject — assigned to teach said course over the years, more or less to a steady drumbeat of often contradictory student criticisms such as "too many concepts to grasp in a short period"; "unnecessarily convoluted"; "too basic and general"; "should focus more on big picture"; and "need to identify specific skills targeted". This, despite significant differences in the various instructors' course plans and approaches over the years. It makes an instructor want to close the final lecture by staring the class down: "If you haven't understood any of this, the problem is not me. It's you." But a better explanation is that the problem is specific to this introductory course, or rather, to the field of policy studies itself, with its dozens of sub-fields and directions in

---

2   See the essay on Global Public Policy reproduced in Appendix A for one treatment of this theme.

the literature that do not always gel well together, and with its disconcertingly open-ended answers to fundamental questions. Once again, it all makes sense in the Latin; public policy's motto must be E Pluribus Unum — *out of many, one* (big mess).

(And oh, the joys of the anonymous student feedback reports that instructors receive at the end of the semester. Instructors love to pretend their skin is impenetrable. Yet informed opinion suggests faculty may respond less defensively to the stinging rebukes of their spouses than to poor student feedback. I should know: The above quotations were taken from student feedback on my round of teaching in the introductory course last semester — an indignity that leaves me speechless. Still, there is no matching the response to poor evaluation scores of one of my former professors at Princeton, who on the first day of the second semester sternly announced the following to his class, which did not take the remark as a joke: "If I see anyone here from last semester's course," — which could not have gone well — "I will spit — in — their — soup.")

A Professional School Without a Profession

This second tension relates to the mission of the School. It is not (the small PhD programme excepted) to produce scholars. It is to promote public service and improvements in governance. To do that, policy schools must have a meaningful relationship to professional practice. But what is our profession? Medical schools train doctors; law schools train lawyers; and business schools train corporate types. What do policy schools train? There will not be a dearth of answers: agency staffers, city managers, NGO activists, governmental affairs officers in corporations, public health researchers — the list goes on.

This raises the question concerning what we want our students to be able to *do* differently or better upon graduation. We want them to have the ability to make better decisions that — under information and time constraints — recognise interdependencies, ethical and other constraints, and that produce sound outcomes on the ground. The ability to "think ahead and think again", as former colleague Neo Boon Siong puts it.

To serve that mission, faculty at the LKY School continue to experiment with a range of ways to make the curriculum more practice-oriented. One is the "policy analysis exercise", in which students essentially write a report addressing a particular real-world client's problem. The end products submitted by students can vary dramatically in quality. Some produce work as brilliant and as practical as that of experienced consultants for hire; some others fail to demonstrate any meaningful integration of the analytical skills targeted in the curriculum. This is partly because it is challenging to get faculty advisors on the same page regarding the "right" approach to policy analysis, and partly (as well as ironically, given that this is another prime way to reach out to the professions) students sometimes neglect their policy analysis fieldwork to pursue more career-friendly (but often less substantive) internships in their summer months. Linking students with diverse motivations and career trajectories to the "profession", in a policy school setting, turns out to be a difficult task indeed.

Global, Asian and Singaporean: All or None of that?

A third tension harkens back to the anecdote at the start of this chapter — the question of whether the LKY School is an "Asian school" of public policy, and what that might mean. Might the School have neglected to build strong and distinctive Asian (and Singaporean) content in the curriculum? The question is superficially plausible. Though some half of LKY School faculty is of Asian origin, virtually all the faculty earned their PhDs from elite institutions in the West — might this bias them against Asian content? The vast majority of textbooks in the field are written with a plethora of Western country examples and cases; could the content of LKY School courses be suffocatingly Western as well? And student comments (again — from those infamous student feedback exercises!) to the effect that "there are too many case studies from Western countries", or that "we came here to study Singapore but didn't find it covered in the curriculum" occur frequently enough to provoke unease (not least in a Dean famed for asking "Can Asians Think?").

Though the above arguments point towards the *plausibility* of an "Asian content gap" in the curriculum, much evidence belies it. In surely one of the more bizarre assessments we have ever completed for the School's management committee, Assistant Dean Eduardo Araral (himself a former graduate of our own PPP) and I assembled a memo in 2010 entitled "How Asian is the LKY School?". The memo presented overwhelming evidence that the School's research, curriculum, faculty and students were neck-deep in Asian content, though not always signposted as such. For instance, the vast majority of research produced by faculty, and a significant percentage of readings in course syllabi, drew on Asian cases or Asian country evidence, even when these courses had titles that were not geographically specific.

Araral and I concluded that the occasional student complaint about Western content in the curriculum reflected the disjunction between many students' prior educational experiences and the pedagogy of a policy school (and at that, one characterised by almost mind-boggling diversity in national origin). Rather than straightforward "answers" to technical questions, students were being exposed to a range of case studies that were meant to be comparative and instrumental. Students might feel understandably frustrated not to see their own country featured more often in the case studies. But that is to some extent beside the point. The important point typically lies not in the *informational content* of the case (whether on Canadian fisheries or the Indian Employment Guarantee Scheme) as in the opportunity it represented to practise linking general themes, generic analytical tools and diverse local contexts.

The Question of Singaporean Content

The issue of Singaporean content turned out to be more complex. Kenneth Paul Tan reflects in Chapter 5 on the unique opportunity the School has to leverage on Singapore's obvious policy and developmental successes as a rich source of analysis and indeed inspiration for the region and beyond. The demand from students and practitioners for in-depth research and documentation on the Singapore experience is also great. For a policy school in this setting, deciding on having a strong Singapore-specific research and teaching capacity is a no-brainer. Yet it may be more difficult to pull off than one might think, for two reasons.

The first is an obvious one: a minority of researchers at the School are Singaporean or predominantly study Singapore. Singaporeans are much better represented on both the faculty and the student body than they were in the "old" Public Policy Programme days, but they still constitute a minority — perhaps 15 percent of faculty and 20 percent of students. It is worth noting that at most other major schools of public policy, it would be more typical for a significant majority of faculty both to hail from, and to conduct research on, the "home" country. In the Singapore context, this is probably not desirable (given Singapore's small size and the global orientation that is the School's unique strength) nor feasible (given the limited albeit growing number of Singaporeans with PhDs in relevant fields), but it does potentially constrain the profile of Singaporean research and teaching at the School.

The second potential constraint interacts with the first and is more subtle. Singaporean governance is perceived by some faculty to be a topic that is sufficiently "sensitive" as to disincentivise them from studying it in depth. I share Kenneth Paul Tan's observation in this volume that he has never experienced even indirect pressure while at NUS to teach (or not to teach) some defence or critique of Singaporean governance. On the other hand, two of my faculty colleagues had, while based at a different local university, an intimidating run-in with the authorities over a piece of Singapore-related research they had written some years ago; and another foreign colleague tells me that issuance of an employment pass for foreigners to work in Singapore comes with the stipulation in the fine-print that one is not to engage in "political activities", something that is left undefined but could theoretically include (for instance) contributions to controversial local policy debates during an election cycle. The fact that this is highly unlikely to be used against someone making constructive suggestions on a given policy domain — say, parking policy — does not mean that academics might not second-guess themselves. In addition, Singaporean agencies are widely viewed by faculty as restrictive in the degree to which they share information on internal work processes and challenges. This may or may not be accurate; it may vary by agency; or it may be changing over time. Regardless, the perception itself may disincentivise work on Singapore.

The end result is that the percentage of "local" content within faculty research and teaching portfolios may be somewhat lower than what one might expect. It suggests the counter-intuitive need for a proactive effort to enhance student understanding and experience of Singapore (a key theme of Kenneth's chapter). And more broadly, it suggests there are subtle and invisible hurdles to overcome for a policy school in Singapore to effectively engage with public policy-making and policy research in its own backyard. I believe the LKY School is successfully navigating this territory, with a growing portfolio of faculty research and courses on Singapore, including much of a critical bend. And the Institute of Policy Studies continues to produce a wide range of excellent Singapore-specific research under the broad umbrella of the School (but with equally broad autonomy from it). Regardless, the issue of the School's relationship to Singapore remains an ongoing challenge — one fully warranting the extensive treatment this subject receives in Chapter 5.

What is the "Global" in Global Public Policy?

Ultimately, the enigma of *what to teach* comes down to giving an answer to the question of what a "global public policy school" needs to address to be relevant in the world today. This was the subject of a colloquium held in mid-2011 at the Rockefeller Foundation's famed Bellagio Center in northern Italy, a quiet place of exquisite, almost soulful beauty nestled in the foothills of the Alps. Dean Mahbubani (who co-chaired the colloquium), Professor Kanti Bajpai (who had newly joined us from Oxford University) and I were the LKY School representatives to the gathering, which included about a dozen policy schools from around the world, all grappling with the same question: How was the changing context of globalisation affecting the curricula and positioning of policy schools?

That the public policy enterprise itself had become more global was patently obvious to the participants sitting around the conference table. The past 10 or 15 years had seen the launch of a rather large number of policy schools in "non-traditional" settings (outside of North America, largely speaking), including Japan, China, Australia, Dubai, Egypt, Hungary, Italy, Germany, India, the UK (with the recent launch of the Blavatnik School of Governance at Oxford University) and Singapore, among others. While many of these schools styled themselves as addressing "global public policy", the term is open to interpretation.

Kishore, Kanti and I put forward our attempt at an interpretation in an essay presented to the gathering.[3] We argued that addressing global elements of public policy and governance was absolutely essential in our changing world. Increasing interdependencies implied that few, if any, elements of domestic or local government

---

3   Please refer to Appendix A, "Global Public Policy as a Field of Study: A View from Asia", by Kanti Bajpai, Scott A. Fritzen and Kishore Mahbubani.

policy could be understood in isolation from broader regional and global forces. The reverse was also true: global governance developments were no longer a matter for only scholars of traditional "international relations". The spaces connecting the local and the global were where real understanding was to be mined. This implied the need for changes in a traditional public policy curriculum. The way in which a handful of global issues and trends were shaping the context of policy-making at all levels — from climate change to demographic changes — might need more explicit attention. Both teaching and researching "global policy" would need to be comparative and multi-level from the get-go. While this may sound obvious, many less diverse, less "globalised" classroom settings tended to fall back onto cases and examples drawn from the "default" national and local set of institutions. This might be understandable where such programmes primarily aimed to train students to enter local administration; but even then, neglect of the global context would hamper the understanding and effectiveness of their graduates. While all the answers have not yet been worked out, we left the conference feeling confident that the institution building and experimentation taking place at the LKY School was at the cutting edge of the "global policy education" question confronting the field.

The Enigma of Whom to Teach

In an "old" PPP/LKY School tradition, faculty have played the predominant role in the admissions process for this diverse student body. After an initial screening by programme managers and faculty, shortlisted candidates are all interviewed in person or by phone by one to two faculty members, for up to 45 minutes. To this end, faculty are flown to several countries in Asia with large numbers of candidates. Following these interviews, a full admissions committee meeting is convened, which culminates after a "mere" 4–6 hours (the meetings are fabled for their intensity and duration) in an admissions and financial aid recommendation for the respective classes.

These marathon admissions committee meetings generate truly heated debates, as faculty wrangle over the merits and demerits of particular candidates and a particular ranking of students within a given country. It is not uncommon for the following to statements to be heard: "I agree that Y isn't very strong academically, but he's extremely well positioned to take off in his career in the Ministry of Z"; or "X doesn't seem to know where her career is going in any convincing way at this point (she's only 23 after all), but just in terms of sheer native intelligence she's someone I would want in my classroom"; or "W has all the attributes we love to see — he's smart, personable, and has senior management experience — but his English test score is regrettable — do you think there's any way that with intensive English training he could get up to speed within the next six months?" These debates, and even some "horse-trading" among faculty vying to get their preferred candidates admitted, tell us something about the odd combination of objective criteria, subjective judgement and school-wide strategising that goes into the selection of a given cohort. (Anyone claiming to have an algorithm or selection process that completely harmonises all these criteria may be selling snake-oil, or *Tongkat Ali*.)

If the question of what should be taught in a school of public policy seems contentious, the question of *whom* to teach in such a school has its own wrinkles as well. As noted earlier, public policy is weakly institutionalised as a professional field; and hence the question of who can and should benefit from the qualification of having a policy degree is not straightforward. A key challenge for the LKY School in its first eight years, then, has been how to define the relevant student target group for each programme.

Growth and Geographical Diversity

To begin with what is more quantifiable, we find tremendous growth and incredible diversity in the LKY School's student body over its first eight years. From its start in the early 1990s until 2002, the Public Policy Programme at the NUS had an enrolment of only some 30 students per year in one degree programme (the MPP); the number was only marginally higher by the launch of the LKY School. But by 2012, the LKY School sported a 350-strong student enrolment, with Singapore, China and India accounting for some 60 percent of the student body and over 50 other countries making up the remaining 40 percent.

This current portfolio of students did not happen by accident; the *kind* of geographical distribution of the students evolved over the course of the PPP and LKY School to suit changing needs and opportunities. The PPP's students came almost exclusively from Singapore's Southeast Asian neighbours; notably there were only a few Singaporeans and Chinese nationals, and virtually no Indians, enrolled in the programme at any given time. With the launch of the School, it was obvious that student enrolment would need to increase to achieve the "minimum efficient scale" that Stavros Yiannouka refers to in Chapter 2. While it would remain important to serve the Southeast Asian neighbours, it was also clear that enrolment in four geographical areas would need to grow substantially: Singapore (to become locally relevant); China and India (reflective both of their tremendous untapped market as well as strategic importance to Asian and indeed global governance); and an open-ended "rest-of-the-world" category (to express the global ambit of the new School). With respect to the last category, it is notable that the number of Americans studying in the School shot up, at least in some years, to the fourth position overall (though miles behind the triumvirate of Singapore, China and India).

By 2008 or so, the standard line we would repeat to ourselves and stakeholders was thus that the school would draw 20 percent of its students from each of the following five areas: Singapore, the rest of Southeast Asia, China, India, and a residual "rest-of-the-world" category. While carving up the world into quintiles seemed to suggest a certain balance, it was always the source of some tension in practice, for three reasons.

First, these targets had a disconcertingly "back-of-the-envelope" feel. It was never clear to what extent they reflected:

- a *de facto reality* (the way the pool of applicants just happened to shape up);
- a well-articulated internal vision of the *desirable* portfolio of students; or
- a qualitative interpretation of what a *"politically acceptable"* distribution of scholarships and students might look like to the school's many institutional and governmental stakeholders.[4]

---

4   The launch of the Chinese-language MPAM degree programme in 2010 surfaced these tensions. Virtually all members of the first two cohorts of this programme have been Chinese nationals, despite some early thinking that the programme might attract Chinese-speaking Singaporeans or diaspora Chinese. Naturally this raised the overall percentage of Chinese among the student body to the number one position, well above the "allotted" 20 percent. The school struggled uneasily with the question of whether it should therefore reduce the scholarships allocated informally to the Chinese contingent of the other two major degree programmes (MPP and MPA).

Second, targeted efforts by the School to achieve a particular distribution of students might always be seen as potentially compromising a commitment to recruiting students *purely on merit*, regardless of their geographical or national background. The fact that merit itself had various connotations in our context — a professional school context with a mandate to train public sector leaders throughout the region — only further muddled the issue.

A final reason was that the mechanics of achieving a target allocation were complicated by the multiple actors involved, and criteria applied, in the student selection process. Attempts to reach a desired balance meant at times uncomfortable interventions by the School's senior management in a process that previously had been almost purely faculty-driven. As a result, in each of the last few years the selection process has been tweaked anew.

The complex selection process demonstrates a simple point. Building a school of public policy from scratch, complete with a distinctive mission and target group, requires years of painstaking "wiring" of plans, procedures and shared expectations. It requires both learning-by-doing and a tolerance of ambiguity in the process.

Diversity in Student Backgrounds

There are other aspects of student composition as well. The employment background or profile of incoming students has changed over time. In the PPP's first decade, the vast majority of the Master in Public Policy (MPP) degree programme students were civil servants from their respective countries. While this is still largely the case for the School's other Master's programmes, the majority of MPP students now hail from the private or "people" sectors, or are recent graduates. The fact that the *clientele* has changed implies also that the product (the curriculum) might need rethinking as well. For instance, the higher number of students with non-governmental backgrounds and ambitions underscores the importance of teaching "governance" from a multi-sector perspective — looking at the myriad ways public and private actors jointly shape development outcomes, rather than focusing solely on what "government" does.

On a more practical level, the changing composition has also placed a strain on the career services of the School. Our predecessor NUS Public Policy Programme had it easy: by and large, students were recruited from their countries' respective civil services, and they simply went back to those services upon graduation. Having become arguably the most diverse policy school in the world (in terms of nationality and sector background), the LKY School has, in contrast, struggled to provide meaningful career advice and outreach to its students. Student grumbling over the school's career services, even as these saw significant expansion, has been a predictable outcome.

These changes in student composition have, in addition, affected classroom dynamics over time. The stereotype of the "argumentative Indian" may be something of an empirical regularity in a classroom setting. The greater number of Chinese nationals led to several sensitive issues: complaints over a "Free Tibet" T-shirt worn by a classmate, or a protest to the School's administration over a Taiwanese student being introduced separately when students from each country were asked to stand up in blocks during the orientation programme for incoming students. The increasing national diversity only heightened the diversity in levels of academic preparation and substantive background knowledge regarding Asian governance that professors could bank on when preparing their lectures.

So the aggregate numbers speak of the diversity of the student body, but how much closer does this really bring us to "solving the enigma" of whom to teach? To go deeper into the question of who can benefit from a policy education, we have to examine the School's five individual degree programmes and their corresponding target groups.

Pre- and Early-Career Idealists, Heading in 50 Directions: the MPP Programme

A first target group describes the current Master in Public Policy (MPP) degree programme at the School. The MPP students have the lowest average age, and the most diversified of backgrounds and interests, of all the students in the School. They are also the most diverse in terms of where they are heading. Relatively small numbers will go, respectively, into government service, the private sector, and further education (perhaps a PhD programme), with a slim majority ending up in a highly diverse "civil society/international organisations" sector.

The MPP student distribution, with its predominance in the "people" sector (as opposed to the private or governmental sectors), is a significant departure from the early days of policy education in the post-World War II period, in which most policy school graduates took positions as policy analysts in government bureaus. The "classic" activities of these graduates — conducting cost-benefit analyses of proposed infrastructure projects, or evaluating the impacts of a given policy to reduce poverty, for instance — were the functions around which much of the curriculum was based. But is anyone actually doing these tasks anymore? The answer is a qualified "yes", in that the contexts in which "policy analysis" is being carried out have certainly diversified. It is probably also fair to note that the number of graduates who are *not* conducting "classic" policy analysis *per se*, but rather are working in a range of positions *around* government affairs — as business consultants, journalists, public relations and so forth — has also vastly increased as a proportion of MPP classes, both here and in North America.

This is a controversial development. On the one hand, purists will bemoan the diversification of careers of graduates outside the traditional public sector as an affront to the policy school mission. In the 1990s, representatives of the family that had provided the large start-up endowment for Princeton University's Woodrow Wilson School of Public and International Affairs sued the university; they wanted their money back. Their charge was that too few of the graduates of the School were moving into the public (in particular, the diplomatic) service. Their ire seems to have been stoked by the perception that none too few graduates were in fact queuing to become highly paid business consultants. The Woodrow Wilson School argued what I believe most in the policy education field believe: that diversified and multiple career paths are here to stay, including in the public sector, and that by implication those who traverse to the private sector upon graduation are neither "lost" to the public for all times nor guilty (necessarily, and in the long run) of neglecting to use their training for the public good, given the manifold ways in which the public and private sectors interrelate in the contemporary world. Yet Princeton settled that case out of court for a princely USD90 million — and the arguments and implications for the field continue to this day.

Professor Robert Klitgaard, former President of Claremont Graduate University, was Li Ka Shing Professor at the LKY School in 2010 and 2011. In a faculty meeting presentation and a public lecture entitled "Speaking Truth to Power: Version 2.0"[5], he put forward a different justification for a diversified approach to curriculum and targets of policy education. The ways that policy school graduates actually make a difference in the real world, Klitgaard suggested, go well beyond the emphasis in traditional policy analysis on finding "*the* answer" to "*the* policy problem". They include, for instance, convening people in unconventional ways, fostering communities of practitioners over time, and reframing policy problems mired in ideological stalemates. Klitgaard calls for a better appreciation of the different settings and ways in which policy school graduates can and do impact upon policy-making and governance.

Controversy nonetheless stalks recruitment to the MPP at the LKY School, in ways that have a bit more "edge" than in the other programmes. One question actively debated in the School concerns "fresh graduates" — those applying right after the completion of their undergraduate programmes. To what extent should they be granted admission? They may be, and often are, academically excellent, in a way (such as through their academic transcripts) that the mid-career students often cannot easily demonstrate. But how sincere are they in aspiring to pursue a career in the public sector? Are they, in the words of my colleague Wu Xun during one admissions meeting, just trying to get a "business school degree on the cheap"? Or are they the avatars of the 21st Century career in public service? The School has blown both ways over the years. In the earlier PPP days, at least a few years of work experience was a hard-and-fast requirement for applicants. With the introduction of the Master in Public Administration (MPA) programme in 2006, an uneasy compromise emerged among faculty for and against taking in fresh grads: up to a quarter of the MPP cohort could be comprised of fresh graduates with no work experience — but decidedly not more. This was not least meant to safeguard the sophistication of classroom discussions, which often depends on students' sharing of their own workplace experiences.

---

5   "Version 1" was a book by the same title (Speaking Truth to Power, Little & Brown, 1979) by one of the great pioneers of the discipline, Aaron Wildavsky.

Mid-Career Civil Servants "On the Move": the MPA, MPM and MPAM Degree Programmes

The three other Master's degrees of the School — in "public administration" (MPA), "public management" (MPM) and "public administration and management" (MPAM) — all cater by and large to sitting civil servants. The MPA, MPM and MPAM are in theory distinguished by the seniority of their students; the MPA students are to have at least five years of experience, while in the case of the MPM and MPAM, a certain rank in government, approximately equivalent to that of a deputy division chief (though titles vary from country to country, and though both may admit a small number of individuals from outside the public sector), is typically required.

The MPA is the flagship mid-career programme, with a cohort some 60-strong inclusive of part-time students, and in its curriculum and structure quite similar to other degrees in public administration. The cohort spends a year studying management, economics, public finance and leadership, during which the students also travel together on a study trip to a foreign country (in recent years, Malaysia, Thailand and Vietnam have all been selected for this purpose). Thereafter, they return to their countries, with most resuming their positions in government (armed with better career prospects); about 30 percent of graduates go into international or non-governmental organisations, and a small number to the private sector.

If the MPA is fairly conventional, the MPM and MPAM degree programmes are almost eye-poppingly unique in the degree-programme landscape. In the MPM, some 20 to 25 students spend half a year taking classes in Singapore. During this time, students also spend several weeks "attached" to a Singapore government agency; under the joint supervision of a faculty member and a senior official "mentor", the students produce an in-depth study of management and policy-making practices of the agency. In the second half of the year, students then travel to the Harvard Kennedy School, where they spend a full semester integrated into the Harvard student body. The experience is capped off with a three day "re-entry" to the LKY School, in which they distil their learning into a presentation for fellow students and faculty. During this experience, this small cohort typically becomes incredibly close, forming friendships and networks that will follow them throughout their careers.

I have taught MPM students several times over the years. The experience offers a unique pleasure. The small size of the class creates an unusually intimate setting, and the rich experience of the student participants can be tapped for fascinating, in-depth discussions and comparative lesson-drawing. There are challenges teaching such a cohort too. Students are even more demanding of practical application and relevance — less tolerant of theory — than their more junior counterparts. That is in some ways a barrier that needs to be overcome. Professor Mukul Asher is the School's longest-serving faculty member, having been "present at the creation" of the Public Policy Programme in the early 1990s. Mukul served too for several years as the lead faculty and guiding light of the MPM programme, always emphasising to successive MPM participants what they most needed to hear — that "nothing is as useful as a good theory". The ability to relate the "war stories" MPM students would bring to the "analytical frameworks" that could help them to understand broader principles is one not every professor (but certainly Professor Asher) possesses.

The MPAM programme, in turn, is taught entirely in Chinese. Launched in 2010 with the strong encouragement of the highest levels of the university, the MPAM may be the only Master's degree offered by a global school of public policy that caters almost entirely to senior officials from another country — in this case, the People's Republic of China. Drawing on the strong desire of NUS President Tan Chorh Chuan and Provost Tan Eng Chye to tap university-wide assets for the programme, the MPAM is jointly delivered by the LKY School and the NUS Business School, and this *per se* adds to the programme's uniqueness. In theory, this set-up should help centre the MPAM's curriculum on cutting-edge issues, such as the design of public-private partnerships in China and beyond. The Business School tie-up accomplished this, while also posing significant coordination and steering challenges in the programme's first year. Coordinating the work of professors has been likened to "herding cats", and the challenges grow when such coordination must cross school boundaries. (Fortunately, our Provost is an excellent herder of cats.)

The MPAM was launched while I was serving as Vice-Dean for Academic Affairs. I was initially skeptical on two fronts. First, how would the arrival of the 60-strong MPAM cohort — many of whom cannot speak English at a conversational level — impact the campus culture? The School's experience two years on confirms that integrating this cohort into the broader student community remains a challenge.

A second concern was whether setting up a non-English-language programme to serve a group of officials from essentially one country was consistent with our brand and indeed our mission to become a "global policy school" with a hugely diverse student body. A turning point in my thinking on this score occurred in late 2011 during a working trip to Beijing. I met with senior Chinese officials of the powerful Central Organisation Department, who carried overall responsibility for the training of Communist Party cadres overseas, and was truly impressed with how well-briefed they were regarding our programme and its curriculum, and by how systematically they had sought out early feedback from participants on the programme's functioning. The internal process for the officials to be nominated for admission to the programme struck me as both systematic and thoughtful, even as it respected the NUS' own standards, selection process and ultimate right to offer or refuse admission. I began to appreciate the special nature of the MPAM and how, seen from a different angle, this unique programme might indeed enhance the brand, diversity and impact of the School.

Aspiring Academics and Policy Researchers

With its annual intake of some five to eight students, the School's small doctoral (PhD) programme caters to students aiming at a career in high-level policy research. The first thing almost every academic in the School does when approached by a bright MPP student wishing to get advice on pursuing a PhD is to try to convince the student to *drop those plans immediately*. Call it a cognitive bias, call it self-delusion — but the fact is that most people eyeing a PhD are rather uninformed as to the risk-reward pay-off. Many are motivated more by an expectation they always nurtured — that they would achieve the highest level of academic qualification possible — than by a realistic need for the degree. Yet the need for sophisticated research on the design and impacts of complex public policies, not least to staff the growing number of public policy schools around the world, provides a justification for having a PhD programme. Another side benefit is the contribution a PhD programme can make to the broader research culture of the School, since PhD students obviously live, breathe and sleep their thesis topics over their five years in the programme.

There was once an active debate among faculty as to whether the School should have a PhD programme, considering the following:

- Is there sufficient demand for the graduates? *(Answer: It's too early to say, but our first few graduates all obtained good job placements in academic institutions.)*
- Were we (in 2007) big enough to support a PhD programme with five to eight students per year? *(Answer: Yes, and having a smaller programme than that would have weakened class cohesion and culture; the "minimum efficient scale" rears its head again.)*
- Should we follow a British or an American model for its curriculum? *(Answer: We began with the former and moved decisively to the latter, which added on a full year of coursework to the mix.)*

By 2012, the programme had come fully into its own, reaching our target enrolment of some 20 to 25 doctoral students. In late May 2012, our latest PhD graduate Michael Raska (now a researcher at the S. Rajaratnam School of International Studies) made an appearance at our monthly faculty meeting to present a bottle of wine to his former supervisor and chocolates from his native Germany for all, simply to express his thanks and appreciation for his experience at the School. From a student, he had transformed into a peer. The PhD programme in any university setting is indeed unique among degree programme offerings in this regard.

It is important to note that the list of "target students" above is not exhaustive. There is plenty of room for diversity. For instance, I have personally interviewed more than a few middle-aged individuals who insisted that the two-year, so-called "early career" MPP was a better fit for them than the one-year "mid-career" MPA. Usually this was on account of a better match between the more technical MPP curriculum and the demands of the individual's job.

Executive Education Participants

There is a final group that must be mentioned. Since the founding of the School, the School has trained, largely using its own faculty, several thousand individuals in short-term programmes lasting anywhere from a day to two months (with a week being typical). The remarkable fact about these individuals is that they are without exception already employed and hence "positioned" to make a difference. This stands in contrast to the degree programmes (especially the MPP), in which we often wait for a whole chain of events — graduates landing relevant jobs and rising sufficiently in their organisational hierarchy and so forth — before we might claim some credit for the impact on the world these graduates are having. If our training programmes could add value to their handling of complex challenges in their various sectoral backgrounds and positions, the contribution of executive education towards our mission might be substantial.

In that "if" lies the core executive education litmus test — for it is not an easy pedagogical task. Time in the classroom is extremely short, and participants often have no preparation or advanced readings for the material they will confront in the classroom. Instructors need to capture participants' attention quickly, hold it, and relate whatever they are presenting to the (real or presumed) requirements of the type of work participants are doing. This must take place entirely in the absence of the typical accountability relationship between each student and teacher (with the latter doling out grades for good "performance"). Quite the contrary: in executive education, the participants are the paying clients (or, as is more common, the ben-eficiaries of paying clients), and hence the accountability relationship is reversed. Indeed, executive education may be the part of a policy school most exposed to a direct "market test" — are organisations willing to pay premium rates on a non-subsidised basis for the product on offer?

My own most unique executive education experience at the LKY School took place in March 2011, when I was invited to give a day-long session in Astana, Kazakhstan to the Prime Minister and the assembled Cabinet of that country. Preparing the classroom at Nazarbayev University, the university officials around me seemed nervous; the stakes in convening this training with such a group were high for the fledgling university. I suspected it would be a tough audience to please; I was told that the whole initiative came expressly from Prime Minister Karim Massimov himself, who was passionate about continuous education and insisted that his (perhaps disgruntled) Cabinet colleagues use a public holiday — and this, two weeks before national elections — to examine "strategic management in the public sector", as well as a day-long session with Professor Asher on "avoiding the middle-income trap".

My attempts to break up a stifling, hierarchical seating arrangement to facilitate group discussions were overridden by a government protocol officer, and after a stiff official photograph the Cabinet took pre-assigned seats in an impressive lecture theatre that doubled as the University's Senate. The next several hours went surprisingly well, as the ministers showed themselves quite ready to engage — to learn from various Asian cases and to critically examine their own policies (the presence of the Prime Minister must have helped on this point).

Such is an example of the magic one encounters at a school with the almost extreme diversity of students such as we enjoy. The opportunity to interact, often within *one's classroom walls,* with students from a few dozen countries — all of whom bring their country, sectoral, organisational and unique personal backgrounds to bear in class discussions — is indeed a unique one for a faculty member. And that brings me to the final "enigma" of professional policy education.

The Enigma of Who Will Teach

I have been asked twice in the past year to provide advice for the development of new schools of public policy, in Russia and Kazakhstan. In both cases, of all the elements I found in play — degree programmes, student recruitment, facility development and so forth — the most important challenge was the development of a strong core faculty and academic culture. I believe, both for these institutions and for the LKY School, that it is the nurturing of a strong faculty base that is, from Machiavelli's memorable phrase, most difficult to take in hand, perilous to conduct and uncertain in its success.

In the case of the LKY School, there have been significant barriers to overcome, for example, in recruiting a critical mass of motivated, high-quality faculty interested not only in building their careers but in building an institution. Or developing, within a research-oriented and increasingly ambitious university, a sense of what excellence in policy faculty means in ways that can be evaluated and used to retain and promote faculty. Over this short but intense period, we have made significant progress in these and other areas, but the road has been far from smooth.

It is impossible for me to look back on this aspect of the School's development without highlighting my own experience, my own trajectory as a faculty member and until recently as Vice-Dean for Academic Affairs; perhaps it may mirror some of the key challenges we have faced.

Special Mission in a Small-but-Cosy Corner of the University: the PPP Days

I acquired a job at the NUS Public Policy Programme a bit like Britain was said to have acquired its empire, in a fit of absent-mindedness. In this sense: it was the very first job for which I threw my hat in the ring, without much thought or hope of success, as I finished my dissertation fieldwork in Vietnam (a period normally too far from PhD completion to be job-seeking). I had seen the position advertised in *The Economist*, and aware that the mother of my Vietnamese fiancée was fully supportive of me marrying her *as long as we stayed in Hanoi*, the thought of Singapore as a negotiated "first step" out of Vietnam for us took root. (In a brilliant move, I later dramatically pulled a map out of my backpack to demonstrate to my fretting mom-to-be that Singapore was actually *closer* to where she lived — at the southern tip of Vietnam — than was Hanoi. I am convinced that I prevailed by the sheer force of confusion caused by that intervention.)

The relevance of this story to the School writ large? None except this (minor) point: I am certainly not the only faculty member for whom marriage and in-laws figured prominently in a decision to move to, or stay in, Singapore. Several of the early (and current) foreign faculty of the Public Policy Programme (PPP) began or ended up with family ties that somehow rooted them here for a period.

Of course, what might bring people like me through the door isn't necessarily what would induce them to "stay and build", as the NUS Provost labels our recruitment strategy. That would be, among other things, the quality of their experience and career prospects here. And those first few years at the PPP were indeed high-quality, memorable years. I remember them as relatively stress-free — a label I would generally *not* associate with career development at the LKY School today, given our ever rising standards for faculty promotion (mirroring NUS' own ever rising star internationally). Somehow, the small number of faculty and students, its lower profile as a low-key *programme* of the Faculty of Arts and Social Sciences rather than the *Lee Kuan Yew* School, and its cosy location atop the sixth floor of the Shaw Foundation Building (with a grand total of one classroom-cum-meeting room), all made for an intimate, almost family-like setting. Even our gossip had a familial ring to it. Would Director Ong Jin Hui force one affable but quick-to-anger faculty colleague to stop bringing his dog to the office? Was former Visiting Professor *X* actually now engaged to our former student *Y*, and who had known that *that* was in the works? And so forth.

This is not to suggest that there were not similarities between the PPP and the current LKY School. The sense of excitement from engaging an amazingly diverse set of students, all of whom had significant work experience, was hard-wired into the programme from the beginning. Indeed, it was even enhanced by the fact that we all knew every student in the programme — and fairly well, at that. Thinking back on what made these early years different, I believe it was this: that the default expectation was that our special mission and scope would, for the foreseeable future, stay roughly what it was at that time. In the LKY School years to come, that expectation was totally upended; the only constant expectation we could have, for several years, was that of change — and change at an accelerating pace.

Faculty Development in the First Years of the LKY School

Where faculty development is concerned, the first few years at the LKY School corresponded for me with a state of heightened anxiety — the anxiety of securing tenure.

In most research-oriented universities, the process of securing "tenure" — essentially, moving onto the permanent faculty as opposed to working on shorter-term contracts — is a qualification process unlike any other. It is essentially a five-year-long "up-or-out" audition for a permanent position on the faculty, failing which one will be asked to seek one's fortune elsewhere. The main criterion is demonstrated potential to be a world-class scholar in a particular field; and the key is to demonstrate research productivity and impact that will be easily recognisable to leading scholars internationally, since they will be asked at the time of the application to confidentially analyse and comment on one's *curriculum vitae*. Not reassuringly, one senior colleague gave me a line I am sure many junior faculty elsewhere have also heard. "No one can tell you," he said calmly and slowly, as if to underscore the point, "exactly what you need to do or how much you need to publish to get tenure." Only later did I discover the statement was largely factual. *No one can tell you*, because decision-making in the tenure-granting process was an almost (on the face of it) ridiculously distributed process — with multiple levels *within* the university and multiple inputs *beyond* the university (among experts invited to comment on one's record) all influencing the result in some unpredictable, non-linear ways.

At the LKY School, the "normal" uncertainties in the process were heightened by the fact that I was the first person to go through the promotion and tenure process as an internal, junior faculty candidate in the new School. Indeed, I recall that in the early days of the new School, there was significant uncertainty among faculty regarding whether the LKY School would tenure *anyone*, or whether it would attempt to make do without this (antiquated?) academic institution altogether. Beyond that question, we wondered what standards and criteria would apply; the first tenure cases would to some extent convey a signal about what *kind* of policy school our stakeholders wanted us to become.

These anxieties specific to the tenure process were a subset of an existential angst among faculty inherited from the early Public Policy Programme days about the way the institution might evolve upon becoming *the Lee Kuan Yew* School. Were we to remain largely internationally oriented in our mission (as was the PPP, with its extremely small number of Singaporean students and faculty)? Research-oriented (like the parent university from which we would be given substantial autonomy)? Critical (and not the "Lee Kuan Yew School of *Thought*"), as Dean Mahbubani had assured us from the beginning? The answers that developed over this period gener-ally conveyed a sense that the School was indeed a "normal" academic institution, where research-active young faculty could reasonably hope to build a multi-faceted academic career.

Entering Early-Middle Age (as a Faculty)

To a large extent because of the answers that emerged, by design and default, to the questions just noted, we had, by the 5th anniversary of the LKY School's founding, entered into a new phase of faculty development. We had demonstrated that the School could be an attractive place for talented junior faculty from all over the world to build a career.

A most encouraging sign of our early success lay in the several junior faculty members who had shown themselves committed enough to its mission to invest significant amounts of time building the School as an institution. We have to date cultivated no fewer than five early- and mid-career faculty members to take up important leadership assignments (for instance, Assistant Dean and Vice-Dean) in the School, including Associate Professor Kenneth Paul Tan, Dr. Suzaina Kadir, Dr. Caroline Brassard, Assistant Professor Eduardo Araral and myself. This is something that would be unusual in other settings, where more senior faculty would normally be assigned such roles. The appointed individuals brought both a sense of purpose and humour to their creative work, creating an energising, collegial environment.

Alongside the faculty lay two human pillars that allowed the academic edifice of the LKY School to expand so rapidly. Agnes Tan (now the staff member with the longest tenure at the PPP/LKY School, clocking in over 14 years) and Ruth Choe (who recently left the School after eight years of service) served as the twin Associate Directors of the Academic Affairs department. Their ability to master the arcane details of degree programme requirements and procedures was matched only by the tremendous personal attention and care they invested in each and every cohort of students. To give a small detail underscoring how unusual their commitment to the student experience was: Agnes and Ruth would travel multiple times each year to Changi Airport to personally greet incoming foreign students, something that (to my knowledge) no other school does at NUS (or elsewhere for that matter). Each year at the celebratory graduation dinner, the loudest student applause — joined by faculty, who appreciated their efficiency, proactive support and congenial manner — was always reserved for Ruth and Agnes.[6]

---

6   The School was fortunately able to recruit an equally capable and dedicated Associate Director — Wu Zhen — for the new Master in Public Administration and Management programme.

In its present phase, the School is confronted by an evolving set of faculty development challenges — challenges that frame our current agenda as a school and which formed the core of my work as the School's second Vice-Dean for Academic Affairs (after Associate Professor Hui Weng Tat, who had laid the foundations) from 2008 to 2011. I will mention just four, though there are many others.

The first is the need to continuously refine our overall academic strategy. We embarked on a participatory exercise to develop a medium-term academic strategy from the bottom-up, with extensive faculty inputs, in late 2008. The resulting road-map focused on a range of quality and process improvements in several areas vital to the impact the School wanted to have on the world. These included: degree programmes offerings and teaching quality, high-impact executive education, support for faculty research productivity, greater cohesion around the School's research centres (a theme covered at length by Astrid Tuminez in Chapter 4) and effective management processes to support innovative institution building. The report document became an important reference point in subsequent updates and reviews, including an important NUS-mandated external evaluation of the School at its five-year mark. Rather than a blueprint, the idea was to develop a flexible approach that could adapt to changing circumstances, a process that continues to this day.

A second challenge is the need to further develop our school-wide performance measurement and management systems. One part of this involves preparing faculty (especially junior faculty) for the tenure and promotion process. Another concerns the annual performance reviews for all faculty. The Dean and I conducted formal, extended conversations with all faculty over a two-month period each year, trying to make the process and results (including the annual performance bonus payments that make NUS somewhat unusual among major research universities) as transparent as possible to the faculty going through the process. In addition, I found it useful as Vice-Dean to have a second, more informal "check-in" halfway through the academic year, to jointly review faculty plans for teaching and research. Though time-consuming, these reviews were important two-way feedback mechanisms, and in a meeting with the NUS deans, Provost Tan Eng Chye cited the School's process as a practice worthy of emulation.

A third challenge is achieving a stable balance over several broad categories of faculty. Until a few years ago, our faculty was heavily weighted towards junior rather than senior faculty; otherwise, we would not have had to rely so heavily on junior faculty to help run the School. Over time, this imbalance has righted itself. In part, we grew out of the problem (with some faculty eventually being promoted with tenure); and in part, we succeeded in recruiting some senior faculty members. By 2011 we recognised a need for *new junior* faculty hires, and in fact made five such hires — from a record 240 applicants — in a highly successful recruitment drive led by one of our new senior hires — Jeffrey Straussman, a former dean himself (of the Rockefeller College of Public Affairs and Policy, University at Albany–SUNY). It was an indication of the growing maturation of our faculty structure.

The balance between practitioners and scholars in the faculty is another classic balance that needs to be struck in any policy school. Generally speaking, we have been successful in hiring a number of "hybrids" — scholars with active consulting practices, or practitioners with PhDs. We have also stepped up our recruitment of adjunct faculty drawn from practising or retired civil servants. Senior adjuncts including Lim Siong Guan, Lam Chuan Leong and Peter Ho among others have taught well-received modules in the degree-granting and executive education programmes of the School. The challenge is to continue to locate and tap such extraordinary individuals, who can go well beyond "telling war stories" to reflecting systematically on their experience as senior practitioners of the craft of public policy-making.

A final, more complex faculty challenge goes beyond the number of warm bodies to staff the School's programmes. It goes to the academic culture and governance of the School. The School has always enjoyed an unusually collegial alchemy — a prime cultural endowment to add alongside the financial, infrastructural and locational endowments of the enterprise. Academic visitors have often commented on an absence of the vicious rivalries and academic politics that characterise some less fortunate departments or schools they are familiar with. And much as faculty may complain about the need to attend our once-a-month faculty meetings, step into the conference room at any random point and one is likely to hear hearty and sustained laughter. Self-deprecating humour alongside affectionate ribbing have long been staples of our faculty culture.

I am convinced this collegiality has had a direct impact on our faculty productivity. For a recent faculty retreat focusing on research matters, we put together a survey to find out who had been working and collaborating with whom over the years, and how this related to tangible research outputs. When mapped out and projected, it became obvious that a key informal grouping of faculty friends led by Professor M. Ramesh — one known for hatching collaborative projects over several rounds of beer into the late hours of the evening — accounted for an impressive share of the School's publications over the years. Shared beer and research output appeared to enjoy a high correlation coefficient — no laughing matter, indeed.

Yet as the School developed from a handful to a couple of hundred administrative staff, researchers and faculty, the possibility of knowing everyone well has of course been lost. Even among the much more manageable number (around 30) of full-time core faculty at the School, it takes more effort to stay engaged than it used to. However positive the "attitudinal endowment" of the School has been to date, it cannot be taken for granted. Yet how do we safeguard it? Like an entrepreneurial culture, attempts to foster it from the top seem jinxed: the harder one tries, the more elusive the goal.

Another element on the "software" side of faculty development relates to faculty self-governance. The School has always had a management culture I would characterise as entrepreneurial, nimble, and centralised: a microcosm of Singaporean governance, one might say. It arguably could not have grown so fast, nor come so far, had it been mired in slow decision-making processes with multiple veto points — a scenario which comes close to describing a number of more traditional academic environments.

Yet academic environments simply cannot thrive long without active faculty participation and empowerment. Some of the most difficult challenges we face as a school — such as growing our research output and footprint; improving the effectiveness of our teaching and distinctiveness of the curriculum; and differentiating between the good and the great in faculty hires and promotions — all require more or less systematic forms of faculty input and self-governance. These are at a nascent stage in the School: present, but needing careful cultivation before we can assure ourselves that they have been "hardwired" into its culture. And they may, at times, sit uneasily with the management culture at the School, which has to date been influenced as much by the high-performance culture of the Singapore civil service, as it has by academic values. In this creative tension of cultures, in the diversity the School harbours, lies a tremendous impetus for innovation. But we still have, to recall Robert Frost's memorable phrase, "miles to go before [we] sleep".[7]

Conclusion: The Enigma of the Field

This chapter has argued that public policy education, here and elsewhere, has a certain enigmatic quality, "a puzzling or contradictory nature", as the dictionary would have it. Public policy is an academic field in its own right, but it is taught mostly by individuals with degrees in other fields. Public policy continues to attract students — I agree with Dean Mahbubani that policy education is a "sunrise industry" — yet there is no denying that the degrees a policy school offers do not guarantee entry into any fixed profession.

Being enigmatic is far from being a weakness, a fatal flaw in the enterprise. At least for me, it has been a great attraction. The attempt which motivates so many of our students and faculty — to *both* interpret *and* change the world for the better — is fundamentally noble and endless in its pursuit. I have invested 12 years of my own professional career to date in the LKY School (and its predecessor programme at NUS) out of a sense that it is unusually well positioned to serve this mission. In no other policy school will one find our level of student diversity. And in few other schools will one find, on the doorstep, so many diverse countries to serve as laboratories of effective or ineffective policy-making. The future prospects for the LKY School to delve deeply and creatively into the many enigmas of the field look bright to me.

---

7   Robert Frost (1923), "Stopping by Woods on a Snowy Evening", in *New Hampshire: A Poem with Notes and Grace Notes* (New York: H. Holt and Company).

4 Richness, Rigour and Relevance: Creating a Strong and Vibrant Research Community at a New School of Public Policy

Astrid S. Tuminez

Prologue: The Best Laid Plans — Opting between a Commercial and an Academic Enterprise

In 2008 I moved to Singapore intending to accept a job offer to run regional public policy and government affairs at Google, Inc. However, before I had accepted the offer, I paid a social call to the Dean of the Lee Kuan Yew School of Public Policy. Two very dear mentors from New York City, where I lived for 13 years, had recommended that I meet Professor Kishore Mahbubani, who had twice been Singapore's ambassador to the United Nations. Not too long into the meeting, the Dean asked me to join the School. He told me that I would have the opportunity to help build a new institution that would educate, train, and inspire Asia's next generation of leaders. Needless to say, I was intrigued.

A good part of my earlier professional life had been spent in international affairs and public policy. I had been an employee and a research fellow at the Belfer Center for Science and International Affairs at the Harvard Kennedy School of Government (HKS) from 1987–1992. For part of that time, I ran the office of the Harvard Project on Strengthening Democratic Institutions in Moscow. HKS was one of the first Western institutions to open an office in the Soviet Union just as the old order was crumbling, and many of the reform-minded elites wanted to work with us. I had the opportunity to work with then-Soviet Foreign Minister, Eduard Shevardnadze and, later, former Soviet President Mikhail Gorbachev; first Russian Chief Judge of the Constitutional Court, Valery Zorkin; the new Minister of Nationalities, Valery Tishkov; and key reformers from government and think-tanks in Moscow. As a facilitator of idea transfers and practical training, I observed how "windows of opportunity" arise in policy, and how exciting it could be when political actors put ideas to the test. At the same time, it was humbling to observe how facile assumptions sometimes blow up in the face of difficult realities; how ideas never neatly translate into practice; and how systems, concepts and practices from one context may not easily transfer to another.

In addition to HKS, I had been a member and Senior Adjunct Fellow of the Council on Foreign Relations in New York. The Council was a hub for thinkers, scholars, innovators, business people, bankers, activists, journalists, and politicians who shared an interest in foreign policy. The Council's staff knew extremely well how to engage the private sector on matters of foreign and public policy, and routinely brought together figures from the public, private, and non-profit spheres to discuss and tackle issues important to public life. Task forces were set up to study pressing foreign policy and domestic problems. These groups' memberships included the highest calibre analysts and practitioners. Their recommendations, as well as other findings from in-house research, travelled widely to opinion-makers, policy-makers, and the general public. In addition, the Council published *Foreign Affairs,* arguably the top foreign policy journal in the world. Its website was also packed with diverse and compelling historical and up-to-date information and analyses of world events, and has been recognised with multiple Emmy awards.

At Carnegie Corporation, where I worked as a programme officer, the heart of our grant-making was "to promote the advancement and diffusion of knowledge and understanding". Andrew Carnegie articulated these words when he established the Corporation in 1911. The Corporation, for over a hundred years, has brought research and knowledge to bear on such policies as higher education, conflict prevention, early childhood cognitive development and learning, and cooperative security. At Carnegie, my portfolio covered US-Soviet relations, non-proliferation of weapons of mass destruction and conflict prevention. I was privileged to see firsthand how knowledge influenced debate, and how ideas disseminated through open means, as well as networks of relationships, could have actual impact on policy. For example, the work done in building relationships between US and Soviet scientists, scholars, and policy-makers for over a decade during the Cold War definitely paid policy dividends when the window for "new thinking" opened under Mikhail Gorbachev.

My years of exposure to public policy and international affairs highlighted for me the qualities of great research from the most influential institutions: richness, rigour, and relevance. In other words, the research had to have solid, reliable and rich data and details; a sound and robust methodology; and resonance with problems and issues at the heart of public life and international relations.

Given my background and experience, I thus found myself wondering, in Singapore, in 2008: what would an Asian counterpart, a parallel, a *doppelgänger* — if such a thing existed — of an American institution of public policy look like? There was only one way to find out: I said "no" to Google and joined the Lee Kuan Yew School of Public Policy.

Our Core Business: Research

Research, teaching and outreach are key pillars of any reputable school of public policy. In this chapter, I will describe the effort and resources that the LKY School has devoted in its relatively short history to build a strong research community. What has the School accomplished thus far, and what are its remaining challenges? The vision in research is that faculty and fellows should produce work that speaks to theory-building, meets rigorous standards of scientific inquiry, and also reflects the richness of data and settings in Asia. Such research would elucidate as much as possible relevant, practical recommendations that would improve policy and its implementation in countries at diverse stages of economic and political development in the region.

In 2011, Professor Robert Putnam, who was then the LKY School's Li Ka Shing Professor, elaborated on research as the "generation of portable knowledge," anchored in sharply formulated questions and solid, testable hypotheses. Putnam urged students to ask why outcomes may not be as they would expect, find strong explanatory variables, and, most of all, be prepared to be surprised. Another Li Ka Shing Professor, Robert Klitgaard, encouraged our School to take on some of the world's (and Asia's) hardest challenges. He underlined the idea that research at the School might take advantage of all the richness of data, settings, attributes and outcomes in Asia. Asia, he noted, provided a great laboratory for social science research. If done well, the work at institutions such as the LKY School should not only produce more solid theories but also identify better policy choices.

Our own faculty and fellows often clarified the attributes of excellent research. The topic is one we discuss often because we are aware that our School is relatively new, young, and small. For the LKY School, the value of great research would be manifold. It would be a *sine qua non* for strengthening the School's academic reputation and consolidating its foundation for longevity and success. Rich, rigorous and relevant research would earn the School the respect of its peers, the attention of governments and practitioners, and the attraction of first-rate students. On the teaching front, research would strengthen the content of classroom instruction and provide the scaffolding on which students could build their own inquiry and hone skills of critical thinking, thorough investigation, and persuasive writing. Research, packaged in different formats for different audiences, would also inform public debates and perhaps even ignite the imagination of the larger public and policy-makers on how and why they might improve or reinvent what they do. Through research, new insights may be uncovered and, normatively and theoretically, such insights could be used to enhance (even if only incrementally) how resources are used and how power is exercised to improve lives and transform Asia. This idea is at the very heart of the LKY School's mission.

The People, the Funding, the Work

When I joined the LKY School in 2008 (the School was just over four years old), the bulk of my portfolio was executive education. However, I was also tasked to spend a fifth of my time supporting research through outreach to Western foundations, oversight of grants administration, and improvement of research dissemination. In light of limited time and resources, it was difficult to balance the two sides of my portfolio. The same dynamic seemed to work at the institutional level, where a demanding research mandate (relevant for tenure and promotions) competed with other compelling demands on faculty and fellows' time. These demands included student recruitment (our professors travelled extensively to conduct personal interviews with shortlisted graduate student candidates from all over Asia); designing a coherent curriculum and individual courses; serving on various committees; teaching and mentoring students; enhancing pedagogical methods and undergoing training; organising and giving campus seminars; teaching in our vibrant and growing Executive Education programme; providing administrative support for a rapidly expanding school; meeting and hosting a heavy traffic of academic and other prominent guests; and so on.

A different approach to research seemed necessary for the School — one that especially clarified expectations and rewards at the outset, was followed through in practice, and complemented by management with a constructive philosophy to "leave the faculty and fellows alone" to carry out their work. But like other matters in a young and rapidly growing institution, human and other resources for such an approach were limited. We needed our professors and fellows to contribute to a diverse range of functions (*e.g.*, student recruitment in other institutions would normally not be undertaken to the same extent as our professors did). Further, the academic and research culture in which we operated, unlike ones I had known in American institutions, required more face time at work and more administrative processes to address different categories of approvals required. These drew time and energy away from research, and sometimes made a few professors less than willing to apply for funding. One of the early insights I had was that patience was a necessary virtue for all our research staff. In addition to patience, we had to be pragmatic and bullish to do what was possible given both our constraints and opportunities.

Who were the people entrusted with delivering on research excellence? When I joined the School, it had more than 40 full-time faculty and research fellows. Like our students, our researchers represented a global community, coming from Asia, Europe, North America and Australia. Many had received their graduate training from highly regarded universities around the world, including the best of the Ivy Leagues. Some had also been affiliated with top think-tanks, such as the Brookings Institution. Thus, our staff clearly had strong research skills and training. We had a handful of senior, tenured faculty, with many more in the junior and middle ranks. Among the younger professors, quite a few still faced the challenge of establishing themselves in research while preparing for their tenure applications within two to five years. The School also had a cohort of adjunct affiliates, but only a few were active researchers. Most tended to be active or retired practitioners, whose value to our community included the wealth of experience that they could share with students in our academic as well as Executive Education programmes. Doctoral students, research associates, and research assistants rounded up our research community.

In 2008, the School had five research centres. The Institute of Policy Studies (IPS), then led by Ambassador Ong Keng Yong, was a mature and highly productive think-tank supported by the Singapore government and recently integrated into the LKY School. IPS already had a long-established reputation as a credible and rigorous think-tank that focused on all policy matters related to Singapore: arts, culture, and media; demography and family; economics and business; politics and governance; and ethnicity, identity and society. It was also privileged in its access to policy-makers and to businesses and other actors that had clear stakes in Singapore's policy landscape. A second think-tank was the Centre on Asia and Globalisation (CAG), whose mandate was to produce policy-relevant knowledge on the impact of globalisation on Asia and Asia's role in governing an integrated world, particularly in the areas of global health, energy, and building markets. For its first four years, CAG was led by Professor Ann Florini, who came from the Brookings Institution. Professor Florini was the author of books and articles on global governance, civil society, and transparency. The School also housed the Asia Competitiveness Institute (ACI), whose staff studied attributes of competitiveness in economic clusters and in countries in Asia. They also investigated how such attributes contributed not only to economic growth but to the actual improvement of living standards. Leading the ACI when I joined the LKY School was a Singaporean, Professor Neo Boon Siong, well known for a book he had written on Singapore, called *Dynamic Governance.*[1]

Additionally, in 2008, the School inaugurated two more research centres: the Institute of Water Policy (IWP) and the Information & Innovation Policy Research

---

[1] Neo Boon Siong and Geraldine Chen (2007), *Dynamic Governance: Embedding Culture, Capabilities and Change in Singapore* (Singapore: World Scientific).

Centre (i+i). IWP, supported by Singapore's Public Utilities Board (PUB), was established to study water policies and governance in Asia and to elucidate ideas and practices on water that would help improve the lives of people in the region. The Institute's founding director, Professor Seetharam Kallidaikurichi, was a senior executive from the Asian Development Bank (ADB) who was seconded to our School. The last research centre, i+i, was established in part to help recruit a professor from the Harvard Kennedy School, Associate Professor Viktor Mayer-Schönberger. i+i's focus was to study the role of information and its impact on the capacity to innovate in markets, organisations and societies. During his time at the LKY School, Associate Professor Mayer-Schönberger wrote an internationally awarded book, *Delete: The Virtue of Forgetting in the Digital Age.*

From my initial vantage point, the LKY School seemed to have the appropriate structure and people for undertaking an ambitious research agenda. The next requirement then was funding. As a former programme officer at the Carnegie Corporation of New York, I was well-acquainted with the power of funding in influencing and facilitating research agendas, and in creating opportunities for dialogue and interaction between policy-makers and scholars. Through Carnegie's funding to think-tanks, universities, and civil society organisations, I observed how scholars and analysts were able to create platforms and a more effective voice for bringing their ideas to the attention of those in power.

At the LKY School, I was immediately struck by the generous support given to research. This was particularly the case when compared with the American context, where proposal writing and fund-raising were constant, thorny challenges, especially for younger researchers and junior professors. In American universities, it was rarely the case for junior professors to receive major, multi-year research funding, particularly with relatively few hurdles in the application process.

The School offered several funding categories that have been, and still are, accessible to faculty and, to a somewhat lesser extent, full-time research fellows. One is the Staff Research Support Scheme (SRSS), which allows research-active professors and fellows to apply for up to SGD15,000 of funding every year. In addition, every faculty member may apply for SGD3,000 yearly to fund participation at a conference to present a paper. Larger funding for individual projects is also available through the competitive Academic Research Funds (AcRF). With a ceiling of SGD75,000, these grants cover up to three years of a faculty member's research. In addition to LKY School resources, the School's parent institution, the National University of Singapore (NUS), through its Office of the Deputy President for Research and Technology (ODPRT), allocates Start-up Grants of up to SGD180,000 (over three years) for new, tenure-track hires. Administered and monitored by the School, these grants constitute a strategic investment in the research of young academics so that they can build a body of work to position them favourably for tenure after six or seven years. Outside of the School and NUS, other sources of competitive funding are available from the Singapore Ministry of Education, other government agencies, corporate sponsors, wealthy donors, and foundations. Numerous grant calls are circulated all the time. The Ministry of Education is particularly generous, with categories of funding above the SGD1 million range for particularly worthwhile and innovative projects. The LKY School Dean, who is a superb fund-raiser, has also many times informed our faculty and fellows that he would find support for all worthy research ideas. In short, on research funding, the LKY School has always been, and still is, in an enviable position.

We have our disadvantages, however. One is that many grant calls within Singapore tend to target science and engineering projects, and projects that have the potential to yield licences, patents, and other output potentially with commercial value. For the social sciences (and public policy, in particular), this is a difficult hurdle. Another, alluded to earlier, is that funding itself without freed-up time to devote to research and writing does not create sufficient inducement. Faculty may compete for funding from NUS to buy-out teaching time, but such funds are limited. Compared to the hard sciences, the social science disciplines usually require more dedicated time for writing and we have yet to develop funding and other support that will free up faculty and fellows' time to focus on writing.

In 2009, my team published the School's first research compendium, spanning the years 2007 to 2009. We featured the work of individual faculty and fellows, as well as research from our five research centres. The compendium captured a rich array of publications and projects — including journal articles, books, book chapters, consultancy reports, opinion pieces, case studies, and working papers.

The compendium also showed that some members of the research staff clearly inclined towards more academic output, while others tilted more towards publications targeting policy-makers and practitioners rather than academic audiences. Some individuals were also clearly more productive than others, with one junior faculty member being hyper-productive, publishing 19 of 25 journal articles and book chapters for the research centre with which he was affiliated during the years under review.

Despite the variation in research productivity and orientation, generally speaking, nearly all the School's faculty and fellows were research active. General productivity was also ramping up. In a 2009 study done by the School's academic team, under the leadership of then Vice-Dean (Academic Affairs) Scott Fritzen, we have the following on record (covering the period from the School's founding in 2004 to July 2009): total journal articles published by faculty increased from 7 in 2004 to 46 in 2009; total Tier 1/Tier 2 publications rose from 4 in 2004 to 20 in 2009; and per capita journal publications went from 0.6 in 2004 to 1.6 in 2009. These measures indicated progress, but the research landscape of the School in 2009 could not yet be characterised distinctively. In other words, we did not yet have a clear answer to the question: What areas of research do we want to be known for — that is, areas where we produce distinctive content and critical mass in output? We had emerging strengths, particularly among faculty who were consistently productive, but both the quantity and quality of the School's research had room to grow.

In addition to people and resources, culture (however amorphous that concept might be) is also an important aspect of any institution's research infrastructure. At my previous places of study and employment (which included Harvard, MIT, and the Council on Foreign Relations, in particular) the love for learning, debate, and discussion (as well as occasional battles of ego, which, arguably, can be routine in academic institutions) was often palpable. A constant buzz surrounded people's research and publications, and those who thought themselves "stars" were constantly trying to outdo one another. The different research communities also prized moments when someone's writings caused a stir in the general public discourse by articulating new compelling concepts or terminology, dismantling or discrediting conventional wisdom, or proposing and supporting startling or controversial insights and conclusions. In our School, by comparison, the atmosphere was — when I came on board — much more subdued. One reason may simply be that the School was a small institution with significantly fewer faculty, fellows and students than other institutions I had known in the US. Faculty and researchers also seemed more reticent (unlike those in America) about overt self-promotion of their research. And perhaps, consistent with general Asian politeness (though we had many non-Asian professors!), not many fiery debates or contention was discernible among our staff.

But juxtaposed against the relatively subdued in-house research atmosphere was the School as a whole itself generating a relatively loud buzz and occasionally frenetic activity in other areas. For example, our Dean and his work on the rise of Asia and the decline of the West, propagated through a popular book and prolific (and, often, provocative!) public writings and addresses, garnered broad global attention. *Foreign Policy* magazine honoured him in 2010 as one of world's Top 100 Thinkers "for being the voice of a new Asian century", and in 2011 as "the muse of the Asian century". Few other deans of public policy schools can claim the singularly intense and effective ways by which Professor Kishore Mahbubani made the LKY School's name a global brand in just a few short years and himself a global public intellectual and much sought-after speaker. In addition to the Dean, outside luminaries often spoke at our School's public events, creating more buzz for the School. A few examples are Paul Volcker (former Chairman of the US Federal Reserve), Tony Blair (former UK Prime Minister), Lee Kuan Yew (former Minister Mentor of Singapore), Paul Kagame (President of Rwanda), Michael Bloomberg (Mayor of New York City), Noeleen Heyzer (Executive Secretary of UNESCAP), Muhammad Yunnus (Founder of Grameen Bank), Elinor Ostrom (Nobel Laureate in Economics), Pascal Lamy (Director-General of the World Trade Organization [WTO]), Sam Palmisano (former CEO of IBM), Deborah Henretta (Group President, Asia, Procter and Gamble), Thomas L. Friedman (columnist for *The New York Times*), Robert Putnam (Professor, Harvard University) and Oliver Stone (Oscar-winning filmmaker). These guests provided a rich menu of extra-curricular learning for our students and community, and significantly enhanced the School's local and international visibility. Compared to the outside luminaries and our highly visible Dean, however, the research voice and impact of our core faculty and researchers seemed faint and at times unduly ignored. In my view, the School needed to support and spotlight better its broad and home-grown intellectual talent and output, and expand the visibility of our larger research community.

Taking Stock: Bricks, Mortar and More

I was appointed as the LKY School's first Vice-Dean (Research) in January 2011, putting in place a resource that was the norm elsewhere in other schools and faculties at NUS. In the process of overseeing and supporting our research portfolio, I have come to appreciate the nuances of both the School's accomplishments and its remaining challenges in research. The School has clearly established the bricks and mortar of a research enterprise (people, resources, structure, process, and output), but a tremendous amount of work remains to be done. And, in some cases (as I will elaborate under "Research Centres" later), the School's management has learned lessons from false starts and incomplete finishes in its research endeavours.

Research Productivity and Identity

The LKY School, now nearly eight years old, can celebrate some quantitative measures of research success. We are trending in the right direction. When we tallied the core faculty's total journal publications, for example, between 2004 and 2009, we found that the articles published per capita for that period was 4.8. By 2011, this cumulative number had gone up to 8.8 (refer to Table 1). Our cumulative academic citation per capita in 2009 (based on Scopus, a citation database used widely by academic institutions) was 40; in 2011, this had increased to 83. Between 2004 and 2012, we had 49 books published by our faculty members and research fellows.

Our research progress is also reflected in five successful tenure applications at NUS, with one full professorship designation, between 2008 and 2012. At the same

Table 1: Research Productivity of School

	No. of faculty	No. of articles since 2004	Articles per capita	No. of books since 2004	Books per capita	Total Scopus citations	Scopus citations per capita
In 2009	28	134	4.8	—	—	1111	40
In 2011	33	289	8.8	40	1.2	2721	83

time, we had two tenure rejections, indicating that we could not be complacent. The School must continue to provide support and expect accountability to help our faculty achieve the benchmarks required at a research-intensive university like NUS, which itself has been rising among the ranks of universities worldwide.

Going beyond numbers, the School still wrestles with its research identity. Are there two or three areas of research in which our faculty should develop and establish particularly deep expertise and coverage? What do we want the LKY School to be known for? Given our geographic perch in Asia, what research areas and methodologies would leverage our distinctive advantages and resources? Do we have the critical mass of researchers needed to develop strong clusters of expertise? General themes in our School's research include governance and public management; economics, finance, and trade; international relations and security; development and development economics; and social policy, urbanisation, and Singapore policy. Within these broad areas, we have emerging specialisation on anti-corruption; the state and its interactions with "new" actors in public policy; conflict and cooperation between China and India; infrastructure, soft power, creative economies, transportation, and other themes related to cities; water, energy and environment; trade, competitiveness, and risk regulation, particularly within the Association of Southeast Asian Nations (ASEAN) region; performance management in the public sector; and healthcare policy, also with a focus on ASEAN member countries. Looking to the next few years, we must continue to strengthen research in our emerging areas of specialisation, and align hiring and other decisions to support these directions. In this spirit, we have inaugurated a new category of funding called Thematic Research Funds, which requires at least three of our faculty and fellows working on the same subject to collaborate. In time, this type of support might facilitate the formation of clusters of deep expertise that will form the basis for a more solid and distinctive school research identity.

To enhance our research culture, faculty and fellows have undertaken new initiatives to strengthen in-house research communication and exchanges. In 2010–2011, we conducted a series of seminars on work-in-progress, giving colleagues the opportunity to present relatively early-stage work. Doctoral students were also invited to participate. These sessions have been useful for soliciting early feedback on the design and implementation of various projects. Another seminar series featured more advanced work — either work already published as books or articles, or research projects being completed — by faculty and fellows. We also organised book launches to celebrate important publication milestones and to recognise publicly the hard work of our colleagues. Further, when we had "star" visitors, we thought of ways to link and spotlight our own faculty's original work alongside the work of these visitors. For example, when Professor Putnam was on staff as the Li Ka Shing Professor, we asked him to chair a seminar in which three of our own faculty spoke about their work on social capital in Asian settings. This generated intellectual synergy between the concepts and data that Putnam knew intimately from Western contexts, and data from original research conducted by our faculty in Asia.

Research Dissemination and Impact

The world of public policy is a "noisy" one. Research, of necessity, must target different audiences and find ways to be heard. Audiences include academics, practitioners, funders, and the concerned public. In my previous work at HKS, I observed many conversations between those who study and analyse policy, on one hand, and those who make and implement policy, on the other. This led me to appreciate the business of research and knowledge dissemination. I noted how entrepreneurial researchers sought to convey knowledge to officials and other decision-makers in the hope that their ideas would have an impact on the world of practice. At HKS, researchers and support staff deployed significant resources to communicate to a broader public the findings and insights of research, and to engage in lively exchanges with those who decide and implement policy.

HKS's culture and people seemed to thrive on being in the trenches of policy and practice, with many faculty members and lecturers alternating between their academic posts and positions in government or multilateral institutions. At the same time, HKS faculty also took scholarship very seriously, producing highly respected books and articles. Indeed, a few individuals at the School had produced seminal and influential works involving theory and concepts in international relations, public administration and management, nuclear arms control, social capital, development and other areas. The professor I worked for, Graham Allison, who was the founding

Dean of the modern HKS (which expanded from a small programme to a major public policy institution under his leadership), had himself co-authored a book that was (and remains) a classic in the field of governmental decision-making and international relations.[2]

In public policy, relevance is a key parameter of research. As one of my thesis advisors at MIT repeatedly put it, the "so what?" question is a critical one. At the end of every research project, the investigator must ask "So what?". What are the policy implications of the data and knowledge generated? What recommendations arise for practitioners and people in the real world? Then the issue becomes one of packaging research in different ways to appeal to multiple audiences; thus, in addition to academic journal articles or books, authors might also do policy briefs, opinion pieces in newspapers, media interviews, essays for magazines, blogs, public seminars and debates, and so on. The idea is to bridge the gap between knowledge and practice — and thus make a practical difference at the end of the day.

In recent years, the LKY School has devoted more attention to developing a diverse array of research dissemination platforms. These include academic journals (the School runs *Policy and Society* and the *Asian Journal of Public Administration*); policy briefs; a quarterly public policy magazine called *Global-is-Asian*; opinion pieces that are distributed widely and translated into Chinese, Bahasa Indonesia, or other languages when warranted; featured research on our School website; uploads on our official Facebook page; the online Social Science Research Network (where our faculty papers have become some of the "most downloaded" and our subscriber base has grown to five thousand and is still growing); and a bi-annual *Compendium of Research*. Through these vehicles, we inform the larger world of the ideas generated by our faculty and fellows and make ourselves active participants in local, regional and international public policy discourse. We also target research dissemination using proprietary, theme-based databases. Thus, for example, if we had a policy brief on energy, we could distribute that brief electronically to a set of local and international analysts, scholars, and policy-makers whose portfolios cover energy.

---

2   Graham T. Allison and Philip Zelikow (1999), *Essence of Decision: Explaining the Cuban Missile Crisis*, 2nd ed. (New York: Longman).

Many of our faculty members participate in direct consultancies and Executive Education programmes with governments and multilateral organisations. These afford them highly visible, direct, and potentially powerful ways to communicate policy-relevant research ideas and findings to a market of policy-makers. These engagements give our faculty a useful reality check because they have the opportunity to interact with, and educate themselves on, the market that a school of public policy is supposed to engage and serve. Some of the School's most visible engagements have included advisory work with the government of Vietnam; multi-year public management and leadership programmes with Southeast Asian governments and governments in the broad Central Asia region (including China, Pakistan, Afghanistan, Mongolia, Azerbaijan, Kazakhstan, Uzbekistan, Kyrgyzstan, Turkmenistan, and Tajikistan); work with mayors and their teams from Asian countries; a multi-year water leaders programme; numerous programmes delivered to Chinese government officials; training for Kazakhstan's Prime Minister's Office; and programmes targeted for Singaporean government agencies and non-profit leaders. Nazarbayev University, a new and promising institution in Astana, Kazakhstan, has also selected the School as its lead partner in developing a graduate school of public policy. Government agencies such as the Indonesian Presidential Development Unit have requested copies of the School's research output to help inform the work that their staff are doing to improve delivery of government services. Our faculty have consulted with senior officials from Asian governments and organisations such as the ADB, IMF and World Bank, and also routinely do press commentary and other media events. We also carry out cutting-edge work such as trends monitoring (with support from the Rockefeller Foundation) in health, energy, and risk management. Tracking publicly available data and data from grey literature, our researchers have generated insights and findings for broad audiences of practitioners from the public, private and non-profit sectors.

The School's magazine, *Global-is-Asian*, has also become a vehicle for disseminating of research in a more accessible format to a global audience, including our peers, media, funders, *alumni* and others. Our editorial policy has evolved towards publishing greater policy content and debate rather than events reporting; soliciting global contributions while retaining the core focus on our own faculty and fellows;

and maintaining an attractive and readable format. We have also increasingly featured the work of our research centres. For example, there is no better source for analysis of Singapore's policies than our own IPS. Thus, the January-March 2012 issue of *Global-is-Asian* featured hard-hitting pieces on Singapore's policy challenges, including more inclusive growth, a new social compact, quality-of-life concerns among citizens, new media and politics, and citizen engagement on the razing of an old cemetery to make space for a highway. Recognising the new communications landscape, we have also leveraged social media, improving our official Facebook page (where we learned, for example, that good, shorter pieces that distil research findings can "trend up" very quickly, reaching potentially thousands of readers and generating feedback and discussion).

Research Support and Accountability

The LKY School created a Research Support Unit (RSU) in 2010 to provide support in grants administration and accountability, research dissemination and impact, and fund-raising. The unit covers work that, in other institutions, would fall under the rubric of communications and marketing, research administration, and development. Working under the Vice-Dean for Research, the small RSU team has created new and improved systems for grants administration, research productivity and impact tracking, more consistent research branding throughout the School and across our research centres, and enhanced liaison with NUS as well as outside stakeholders and funders. RSU also fully supports the work of the School's Faculty Research Excellence Committee, which reviews all research proposals from faculty and fellows and makes funding decisions. Since the inception of RSU, a more predictable and disciplined process has been implemented to review grant applications, notify successful applicants, and track outputs and outcomes. This may appear trivial at first, but organisationally, such processes help us strengthen research support and promote the ethos of systematic reviews and accountability. RSU has also supported successful grant applications to funders including The Rockefeller Foundation, Sloan Foundation, the Centre for Strategic Futures in Singapore, NUS ODPRT, and the Singapore Ministry of Education. These external grants have opened avenues for collaboration and research on resonant and promising themes, including trends monitoring in Asia, conflict and cooperation between China and India, women's leadership in Asia, and science engagement in South Asia.

Research Centres

Research centres, whose directors and fellows work full-time on policy-relevant research, can make important contributions to public policy education and practice. Calling these "problem-solving research centres", Graham Allison elaborates on their role to include "developing solid databases, sorting the facts, analysing the options, and raising the level of governmental and public discussion of major public policy choices."[3] He notes also that the reluctance of traditional university departments to take on the role of serious public problem solving was no longer an affordable option. Therefore, research centres must fill the gap. When the LKY School was founded, the consulting firm that assisted in its strategic planning highlighted research centres as a key component of top public policy institutions. Thus, to be consistent with best practice in more established places, the School set up four new, and incorporated one extant, research centres (mentioned earlier). To date, the centres have had important successes. The Institute of Policy Studies (IPS), having had a long history prior to the LKY School, remains the go-to think-tank for understanding key factors and dynamics in Singapore's policy landscape. Its landmark annual conference, *Singapore Perspectives*, has always drawn a large audience, and its research continues to shed light on Singapore's policy successes and evolving challenges.

The Institute of Water Policy (IWP), established in 2008, has published many edited books, special issues of journals, book chapters, working papers and opinion pieces. Highlights include special issues of the journals, *Water Policy* and *International Journal of Water Resources Management* and a contribution in 2009 to the flagship report of the Asia Society on Water Security in Asia. This was the first report given to the Obama administration. In 2010, the first Asian-generated monograph of its kind, *Index of Drinking Water Adequacy*, was launched during the Singapore International Water Week (SIWW). In that year, IWP also started a

---

3   Graham Allison (2006), "Emergence of Schools of Public Policy: Reflections by a Founding Dean", in Michael Moran, Martin Rein and Robert E. Goodin, eds., *The Oxford Handbook of Public Policy* (Oxford, UK: Oxford University Press), p. 72.

book project, *The Singapore Water Story*, which is expected for publication in 2013. This book will elucidate Singapore's remarkable success in water management in a context of relative water scarcity. Another milestone was the launch in 2010 of the *Asia Water Governance Index* (AWGI) by the late Nobel Laureate, Elinor Ostrom. AWGI was the result of research efforts led by faculty member Assistant Professor Eduardo Araral.

With generous funding from Dr. Seng Tee Lee, the Centre on Asia and Globalisation (CAG) in its first years published two special issues of the *Global Policy* journal, focused on global energy governance and global health governance. In addition, the centre convened key experts from all over Asia to publish an edited book on global health governance, addressing the role of Asian countries as donors in global health, as contributors to collective action instruments to address global health challenges, and as participants in governing global health research and knowledge production. CAG's research fellows also published books and articles on transparency and governance, regional development, social movements, new actors in market formation, risk and regulation, energy security and energy governance. Most of this research was governed by the overarching goal of elucidating how evolving norms and institutions of global governance exert an impact on Asia and how Asia, in turn, influences these norms. CAG's work under its first director, Ann Florini, helped create an early global epistemic community around the themes of global governance in health and energy.

The Asian Competitiveness Institute (ACI) in its first years published competitiveness reports on Vietnam, Singapore and the ASEAN region. Its first director, Professor Neo Boon Siong, together with Professor Geraldine Chen, wrote a particularly enlightening and influential book on Singapore's public governance. Entitled *Dynamic Governance: Embedding Culture, Capabilities and Change*, the book has enjoyed popularity among the many international government officials and civil servants who participate in the LKY School's Executive Education programmes. ACI's research has also focused on China and Indonesia, addressing in particular China's role as a regional engine of growth and examining competitiveness factors at the provincial level in both countries. The Institute's potential remains in generating proprietary data and original insights on competitiveness in the ASEAN region and in Asia in general.

The centres' successes have been meaningful, but in 2009–2010, the School recognised some problems related to leadership alignment between some of the centres and the School. Individual centres had different problems; these included snags in funding, lower-than-expected research performance (in some cases where funding was plentiful), weak mentoring of junior researchers, misaligned designations and actual duties in administration and research, and the formation of institutional silos. Staff pruning, leadership change and, in one instance, closure of a centre, followed. Difficult lessons surfaced, including the need for the School's management to ensure that centres were aligned and integrated with a one-school agenda and were more accountable for performance and resource use. Individual centres also needed to do more to integrate full-time faculty into their work, given the small size of the LKY School and the difficulty of hiring qualified research staff even when funding was available. Another lesson had to do with managing better the tension that arises when funding is short-term, but the mandate for a centre runs through the medium- to long-term — that is, to build a core cadre of professional policy analysts and establish a distinctive and distinguished research agenda and reputation. On accountability, standards of excellence and expectations must be articulated clearly and followed through. Finally, the School learned that it was unwise to create a research centre to recruit one professor. Similar to what is called a "key man" in venture capital deals, the departure of such a person could become a deal-breaker. Thus, when the Director of our Information & Innovation Policy Research Centre decided to move to Oxford, the centre he headed became unsustainable.

The problems encountered by the LKY School with regard to research centres are hardly unique. Work is still evolving, and it remains to be seen how the lessons of the past, new leadership, new research agendas and support from stakeholders (including those in the Singaporean government) will evolve to guide the centres' future productivity and impact of the School. One thing is certain: The work of the centres will have a bearing on the School's growing reputation; therefore, we must continue to strengthen our stewardship of the people and resources devoted to research within them.

Through the Looking Glass . . .

The LKY School, although only eight years old, has already made remarkable progress as a new global school of public policy located in Asia. In the research area, the School has to reflect on at least four critical areas as it seeks to improve its research strategy and outcomes.

People, People, People

In reflecting on his years as "founding dean" of the HKS, Graham Allison states that core faculty is essential. "A small number of quality people can set the tone. Commitment is contagious . . . The five criteria adopted by the faculty and applied . . . are: 1) quality of mind; 2) research and written product; 3) teaching; 4) demonstrated attainments in public policy and management; and 5) institutional citizenship."[4]

Recruitment is never a simple matter even when you have a wide recruitment pool such as in the United States. For the LKY School, the challenge is thornier because its recruitment pool is constrained by the School's location in Singapore. As wonderful as this city-state is for those of us who know it well, it is nonetheless not a guaranteed magnet for more established faculty in larger markets such as the US or Europe. The School in 2012 undertook an intensive faculty recruitment exercise and was able to recruit successfully six new faculty members, five of whom were new PhDs from some of the top schools in the US. The School must prioritise mentoring of new faculty so that they could progress consistently and systematically in their research and scholarship. They must be given the right support and informed of expectations so that surprises (especially negative ones) may be avoided down the road. Support must also include devising ways to attract and retain qualified research assistants. Again, because of a smaller research and academic market in Singapore, our researchers have often encountered difficulty in finding qualified research assistants and associates, sometimes contributing to months of delays for research projects.

---

4   *Ibid.*, p. 76.

Management to Support Research

A useful practice for our School's management is to consider how to avoid distracting the people who do research. This means minimising administrative loads, especially for younger faculty who are building their research portfolios towards tenure. Standards and incentives for research excellence also need to be clarified, and implemented with discipline. Rewards should be distributed in more predictable and transparent ways to encourage faculty and fellows who may not always feel that they understand the reward structure for research. Management can also support and encourage more entrepreneurial approaches in communicating research to consumers and patrons (including foundations, multilateral institutions, governments, media, and opinion-makers in public policy). Finally, administrative processes for research approvals, hiring, field research, reimbursements and others need to be simplified so that researchers could focus on their work and not be daunted by the amount of bureaucratic hurdles they must surmount.

Convening, Publicising, Pushing the Boundaries

One of the powers of a public policy institution, especially one that enjoys great prestige like the LKY School, is to convene thought leaders on pressing policy issues. An example alluded to earlier are the task forces that the Council on Foreign Relations in New York City sets up to address pressing policy issues. When the global financial crisis ensued in 2008, the LKY School used its convening power to organise a Task Force on Asia and the Global Economic Crisis. Comprised of academics and practitioners (Asians, Americans and one European), the Task Force wrote a report on the causes and implications of the crisis for Asia. Although impact was limited, the exercise was nonetheless a small step in learning to be nimble in addressing burning policy questions that concern Asia. Otherwise, the definition of such matters will rest, as has been traditionally the case, with Western think-tanks and researchers and we will lose out in terms of framing issues and underlining key findings on matters right in our own backyard.

What are the big policy issues in Asia? What matters the most for improving governance and alleviating poverty and hardship in individual countries? What works where in infrastructure, taxation, poverty alleviation, health policy, defence and security, gender equality, budget transparency, sustainable development, and other areas? Our School has to sustain support in all these areas of research, many of which our faculty are already addressing. A challenge in Asia may be that policy debates are not as lively as they are in Western societies. The culture is more polite, and deference to authority (that is, government leaders) is valued. In this context, style and modalities are important. The School, through its convening power and prestige, can help facilitate critical (yet polite and constructive) policy discussions between researchers and policy-makers. It remains to be seen if the School can succeed more in this enterprise. Asians may never welcome American-style "in-your-face" policy debates, but there is room to bridge the gap between knowledge and practice. As Asian countries become more affluent and more visible on the global stage, the boundaries of policy discussion, criticism and debate may well enlarge. The School will have its role in pushing these boundaries.

At home, in Singapore, the LKY School must also engage policy-makers in important ways. Research and benchmarking are second nature to the Singaporean government. As one of the most efficient governments in the world, Singapore has much to teach others in the policy arena. How can our faculty and fellows partner with government, get data, and still retain academic control and independence in publishing? In science and technology, for example, the Singapore government has made huge investments, but our own research has not adequately addressed this area. As a school, how can we find effective ways to convince government agencies to share "sensitive data", do our research, allow our government partners to review manuscripts, and yet give academics the final say on publishing? What value can we offer to the government? Would it be in generating compelling case studies of Singapore's management success, showing not only the successful endpoints but also perhaps any failures, missteps, debates and challenges along the pathway to success?

A Market-Sensitive Portfolio of Big and Incremental Ideas

Asia provides scholars and analysts with a great laboratory for comparative policy research. Policies and settings vary widely among countries in the region. Asia's rich policy setting could facilitate studies that lead to better theories and better policy choices. The School, for example, could generate unified data sets for comparison among countries and build a new course on comparative research. Going forward, the School's research will continue to evolve as a portfolio: some of it covering big questions across countries, and some covering in more incremental ways the details of policy in smaller settings. The portfolio will also include more theory-oriented work and more applied studies that examine concrete policy and practice. As this portfolio evolves, the School must remain "market-sensitive". What this means is that we have to remind ourselves constantly that we do have a public role and purpose. We need to contribute to education and to public debates. We must continue to forge strong and open relationships with governments, foundations, civil society, and other stakeholders. We must prove and sustain our relevance. As Professor Stephen Walt, a veteran participant in American and global public discourse, has argued:

> . . . it is highly desirable for university-based scholars to play a significant role in public discourse about key real-world issues and to engage directly with policymakers where appropriate. . . . [Academic] research can provide policymakers with relevant factual knowledge, provide typologies and frameworks that help policymakers and citizens make sense of emerging trends and create and test theories that leaders can use to choose among different policy instruments. Academic theories can also be useful when they help policymakers anticipate events, when they identify recurring tendencies or obstacles to success, and when they facilitate the formulation of policy alternatives and the identification of benchmarks that can guide policy evaluation. Because academic scholars are free from daily responsibility for managing public affairs, they are in an ideal position to develop new concepts and theories to help us understand a complex and changing world.[5]

---

5   Stephen M. Walt, "International Affairs and the Public Sphere", http://publicsphere.ssrc.org/walt-international-affairs-and-the-public-sphere/ (accessed 23 April 2012).

In *Lieu* of a Conclusion

Is the LKY School positioned for success? Have we taken on the hardest, most pressing policy problems? Do we have the people and the motivation to excel in research and to bring policy debate and engagement in Asia to a higher level? The School has not yet "arrived", and it may well be *naïve* (or even arrogant!) to assume we would any time soon. However, the reality is that the School has tremendous resources at its disposal to achieve greater things in research productivity and impact. The key to future success includes sustained commitment and the right motivation. Our faculty and fellows, like everyone else, may be motivated by potential fame and commercial success (even in the social sciences, bestselling authors can become media figures and earn lucrative speaking fees!), and by the perks of professional advancement (tenure, pay, and titles). But, as Henry Rosovsky, the former dean of the Harvard Faculty of Arts and Sciences, notes, we should strive for more:

> *Research is an expression of faith in the possibility of progress. The drive that leads scholars to study a topic has to include the belief that new things can be discovered, that newer can be better, and that greater depth of understanding is achievable. Research, especially academic research, is a form of optimism about the human condition.*[6]

If the School can subscribe to this ethos, our research will undoubtedly keep improving and we will, indeed, as stated in our mission, do our share to improve lives and transform Asia.

---

6   *Op. cit.*, p. 89.

5 A "Singapore School" of Public Policy

Kenneth Paul Tan

Over the decades since Singapore gained independence in 1965, its practice of policy-making has gradually been codified into distinctive principles and retold through narratives that circulate in the public sphere — mostly unchallenged — as The Singapore Story.

The process began as a defence against liberal criticism from the West, evolving into an effort to identify success factors for a model of development that could serve both as fundamental principles to steer Singapore forward in more complex times as well as a source of inspiration and techniques for other developing countries looking for lessons. Today, the Singapore model seems to be receiving positive attention and even admiration from political leaders and policy-makers in both developing and advanced countries. The Singapore model is, thus, a short way from becoming a national brand.

At the same time, Singapore's soft-authoritarian political environment, which shapes the possibilities and limitations of policy-making, has evolved. There are new policy challenges and a more variegated citizenry motivated by different needs and aspirations. Ironically, the People's Action Party (PAP) government's success has created a more globally conscious, capable, demanding and articulate citizenry. Encouraged and stimulated by activities in alternative media platforms, and influenced by intellectuals and mobilisers, citizens have become more willing and able to challenge government decisions and, to a degree, even the legitimising assumptions underlying them. The strong state that has enjoyed high levels of autonomy and insulation from popular pressure looks as if it will transform to cope with and make the best of more expansive practices of public participation and the prospects of more competitive elections.

In this chapter, I reflect on the Lee Kuan Yew School of Public Policy's place in this larger political trajectory and its role in the codification of Singapore's practice of policy-making. Specifically, this chapter presents a perspective on the tension between deep engagement and critical distance, both necessary for the LKY School to be a relevant and credible force in ensuring that Singapore's policy-making practice remains dynamic and self-reflective.

I write these reflections as a scholar and educator on Singapore's politics and culture, the School's Vice-Dean (Academic Affairs), and the former Assistant Dean in charge of student affairs and a co-curricular programme called The Singapore Experience@The LKY School, conceptualised as a beyond-the-classroom programme designed to give students and faculty different opportunities to interact with Singapore's leaders in the public, private and non-profit sectors. From this vantage point, I will discuss aspects of the School's broader educational role and the needs of its students (mainly in terms of curriculum and pedagogy) and the avenues by which faculty members engage with Singapore policy-makers (such as consultancy projects, executive education, research and publications, media commentary, and the employment of adjunct professors). In all of these aspects, a central challenge has been finding the right balance between policy intervention and critical distance, as well as practice and theory.

Codifying the Singapore School of Policy-making

Practices that are deemed successful tend eventually to become codified. As an introspective project, the codification of Singapore's public policy experience serves to identify the basic reasons and circumstances that have enabled success, to understand the internal weaknesses and environmental challenges in the near future as well as distant horizon that could threaten continued success, to reproduce this success with some optimism and a sense of pride, and — at a more advanced stage — to question the very basis of what counts as success and to offer alternative means of achieving it.

The process of codifying a "Singapore School" of policy-making began in earnest shortly after the end of the Cold War, when the triumphant West transferred its attention away from the "communist threat" to regimes in mostly developing countries that did not measure up to the human rights standards proposed by a growing liberal democratic global hegemony. Singapore, naturally a target of this criticism, responded mainly through the voices of public intellectuals associated with its diplomatic establishment. Whether it was the measured and gentler voice of Professor Tommy Koh (currently Ambassador-at-Large and Special Advisor at IPS) or the more strident and challenging tones of Bilahari Kausikan (currently Permanent Secretary, Ministry of Foreign Affairs) and Kishore Mahbubani (currently Dean of the LKY School), the words of Singapore's defenders in both speech and print effectively systematised Singapore's policy-making practice in contra-distinction to what was often (and certainly not always) a caricature of a culturally and politically degenerate West, accused of imposing — in neo-imperialistic terms — its values and institutions of liberal democracy.

Their message was clear and pointed. In essence, they argued that individual, civil and human rights were a specifically Western construct that should not — whether out of ignorance or a desire to dominate — be imposed upon the non-West in ways that ignored its particular as well as diverse historical, cultural and social circumstances. Singapore, they argued, valued social stability and economic growth above all other collective and individual goals, given its historical vulnerabilities. And Singaporeans' "Asian values" put the nation, the community and the family above the individual. Similarly, citizens' duties and responsibilities ranked above their political and civil rights.[1] This "self-orientalist" strategy — coupled with an equally potent strategy of "occidentalising" the West as an inefficient, deadlocked, corrupt and self-centred political society — contributed greatly to the early formation of an ideological alternative to Western liberal and human rights discourse. Their efforts were buoyed by the rising confidence and assertiveness of a region

---

1   Melanie Chew (1994), "Human rights in Singapore: perceptions and problems", *Asian Survey*, 34 (11), p. 937.

that witnessed social stability and rapid economic growth in several countries with strong and authoritarian states. The market, it seemed, could prosper just as well, if not more impressively, when coupled with judiciously expansive state intervention. The process of codifying a Singapore school of policy-making, therefore, began as a defensive rather than an introspective project.

The late 1990s witnessed the emergence of The Singapore Story, in part the product of a "national education" campaign addressing a top-down concern that the younger generation of Singaporeans were unacquainted with their historical vulnerability as a nation and therefore less appreciative of the PAP government's role in ensuring continued survival and success. The Singapore Story, a victor's history, is unavoidably ideological. In this official national narrative, founding father Lee Kuan Yew is cast as the heroic protagonist, his PAP colleagues placed in supporting roles, and his political opponents portrayed as antagonists. Chief among these documents have been the massive two-volume memoirs of Lee Kuan Yew, the first of which in fact bears the title *The Singapore Story*.[2] Each volume is prefaced with several pages of congratulatory and flattering remarks offered by the most prominent political and thought leaders on the global stage. A more recent book, subtitled *Hard Truths to Keep Singapore Going*, was based on interviews with Lee, who had expressed a wish "to educate [the young generation] on the hard truths about their country and why it needs an exceptional approach to government".[3] Not only has The Singapore Story narrativised the Singaporean values of meritocracy, pragmatism and corruption intolerance, providing cultural and ideological resources for thinking about and justifying nearly all policy decisions taken, it has also become the scriptural basis of reverence for the founding father within the policy establishment.

Singapore's Civil Service College was established in the 1970s mainly as a training institute for public servants. In more recent years, it has evolved into a centre whose mission includes being "actively involved in circulating, validating

---

2   Lee Kuan Yew (1998), *The Singapore Story: Memoirs of Lee Kuan Yew* (Singapore: Times) and (2000), *From Third World to First: The Singapore Story: 1965–2000* (Singapore: Times).

3   Han Fook Kwang, *et al.* (2011), *Lee Kuan Yew: Hard Truths to Keep Singapore Going* (Singapore: Straits Times Press).

and renewing knowledge with practitioners in government and external partners" and connecting "the Singapore Public Service to external perspectives through forging strong networks with leading institutions and thinkers in the area of public governance both locally and globally, as well as industry players and academic institutions".[4] The College runs lectures and courses, and produces a journal, several newsletters and case studies that constitute an important part of larger processes that shape the discourse on policy-making in Singapore. A recently published volume of speeches is described in its introductory pages as part of "ongoing effort by the Civil Service College to document the evolution in thinking and philosophy behind many important public sector initiatives over the past decade".[5] The volume's aim of eliciting "deeper reflection among public officers about the core values and principles that underpin our mission; the challenges and demands facing the Public Service in the 21st Century; and what we need to do to be in time for the future", and its emphasis on "keep[ing] pace with a fast changing external environment and with increasing customer and citizen expectations", highlighted how important it was for the policy establishment to reflect and adapt as circumstances evolve.

This adaptive quality is a feature of Singapore's pragmatic mode of policy-making. Part of the Singapore success story must be attributed to its conscious efforts to learn and adapt best practices from anywhere in the world. As Prime Minister Lee Hsien Loong explained recently, "Up to now, Singapore has had the benefit of following and adapting best practices by others who are ahead of us." Lee also noted that Singapore was moving "closer to the leading edge" and therefore needed "to break new ground ourselves, find fresh solutions and feel our own way forward".[6]

The fact that Singapore is at — or close to — this leading edge in policy-making is evidenced by the continuous stream of overseas delegates and officials who visit Singapore in order — as they themselves admit — to learn something about

---

4   Civil Service College, "Mission, vision, values". Homepage at <http://www.cscollege.gov.sg/page. asp?id=24> (accessed 27 April 2011).

5   Donald Low and Andrew Kwok (eds.) (2009), *In Time For The Future: Singapore's Heads of Civil Service on Change, Complexity and Networked Government: Speeches by Lim Siong Guan and Peter Ho* (Singapore: Civil Service College).

6   Quoted in Peh Shing Huei and Chin Lian Goh (2007), "Life on the edge", *The Straits Times* (Singapore), Saturday Special Report, 7 April.

Singapore's experience of rapid development from a third-world post-colony poor in natural resources to a first-world nation whose per capita GDP ranks among the highest in the world. Former PM of the United Kingdom Tony Blair noted how, in his travels, he often encountered national leaders who cited Singapore as a model for their development.[7] Although Lee Kuan Yew remains generally pessimistic about whether other countries can copy the Singapore model, given its unique history and circumstances,[8] opinion-leaders in the advanced world have also pointed to Singapore as an exemplar. Thomas Friedman, writing in *The New York Times*, encouraged his fellow Americans to learn from Singapore's attitude "about taking governing seriously and thinking strategically".[9] Noel Pearson, writing in *The Australian*, urged policy-makers in the Cape York Peninsula not to focus only on the US and Britain for ideas in the area of welfare reform. Singapore, he argued, offered an example of how redistribution could be achieved by improving "the asset and wealth development capabilities of its citizens", specifically through its system of compulsory savings and universal home ownership.[10] A special report in *The Economist* praised Singapore's highly qualified and meritocratic government, arguing that:

> ... *the place that should be learning most from Singapore is the West. For all the talk about Asian values, Singapore is a pretty Western place. Its model, such as it is, combines elements of Victorian self-reliance and American management theory. The West could take in a lot of both without sacrificing any liberty. Why not sack poor teachers or pay good civil servants more? And do Western welfare states have to be quite so buffet-like?*[11]

As discussed earlier, the process of codifying the Singapore school of policy-making began as a defensive activity against criticism from the liberal West. It then

---

7   Quoted in Kishore Mahbubani (2009), "The republic of common sense", *The Straits Times* (Singapore), 9 September.

8   Leonard Apcar, Wayne Arnold and Seth Mydans (2007), "Excerpts from an interview with Lee Kuan Yew", *The New York Times*, 29 August.

9   Thomas Friedman (2011), "Serious in Singapore", *The New York Times* (US), 29 January.

10   Noel Pearson (2011), "Proof of welfare's multiple failings", *The Australian* (Australia), 5 March.

11   "Go East, young bureaucrat", *The Economist*, 17 March 2011.

developed into a means of consolidating national self-knowledge, became figuratively a "textbook-in-the-making" of good governance for developing and advanced countries, and is now on its way to becoming a national brand.

Evolution of the Political Environment

In their opinion pieces, both Friedman and Pearson acknowledged that, while Singapore offered lessons to learn, it would be unrealistic (and probably undesirable too) for their respective countries to adopt Singapore's authoritarian and paternalistic methods. Although this observation was really a reference to the deeply entrenched liberal values of mature democracies, it is a crucial point that speaks to the very possibility of policy transfer and of learning anything at all from authoritarian Singapore's experience. It could be argued that Singapore's policy success really hinges on its government's ability to implement good ideas and not just to come up with them. Just about any country that is able to attract enough talent into its policy establishment can formulate impressive policy ideas. But few democracies that seriously pay heed to the range of powerful and often conflicting interests in their societies can actually put these ideas into practice without some amount of resistance, obstruction and compromise. Policy-making talent alone is necessary but insufficient for successful implementation that can yield desirable outcomes. All of this, it might be argued, could be reduced to the simple proposition that Singapore succeeded because it had a dominant-hegemonic one-party state, largely insulated from popular and party-political pressures.

Such a proposition, however, needs to be understood in historical context; and Singapore politics needs to be seen as not static but evolving and complex. Historically speaking, the strong Singapore state in the 1970s and 1980s played a powerfully directive role and was insulated from and yet embedded in the economy and society. Along with countries like Japan and South Korea, Singapore was described in the "developmental state" literature as having a rapidly-industrialising economy, growing at an accelerated pace towards advanced and high-income status, all within a couple of decades. It is difficult to argue against the claim often made that Singapore needed authoritarian government led by the draconian instincts and methods of its first prime minister, Lee Kuan Yew, during a time when vulnerability and lack threatened the newly-independent nation's prospects for survival. Today, countries at the lower rungs of the development ladder will be extremely interested in assessing this earlier phase of Singapore's development to see what aspects of this might work for them, what might not, and what will not be seen as legitimate in the contemporary discourse on international human rights, which they cannot afford to ignore.

But Singapore's politics has also been described as undergoing a gradual process of liberalization. The tough and no-nonsense characteristic of Lee Kuan Yew's rule from 1959 to 1990 gave way to the kinder, gentler and more consultative style of his successor Goh Chok Tong. When Lee Hsien Loong took over as Prime Minister in 2004, the same year that the LKY School was established, he announced that Singapore should become more open, diverse and inclusive as a society of active citizens, one that made room for unconventional thinking. To a degree, this loosening up has been a function of an increasingly affluent, educated, globally connected and media-savvy citizenry, with rising expectations of a government that has set a high bar. Deeper participation in globalisation (of the neo-liberal capitalist kind) has also resulted in emergent political challenges, including more frequent economic crises, rising cost of living, growing economic and social inequalities, and social frictions caused by liberal immigration policies.[12]

However, this slow process of political liberalisation continues to be marked by strong state intervention and actions that can easily be described as authoritarian, if not strongly paternalistic. This should not be surprising: These anachronistically harsh political moments in Singapore's more liberal present are a legacy of the developmental state in the earlier decades, whose strong state institutions have become embedded and entrenched, their scope and capacity to maintain economic success jealously guarded.[13] Ironically, the neoliberal global city that Singapore is today requires just as strong a state to maintain social and political stability by policing fragmenting forces that can mobilise around crises, inequalities and divisions.

---

12 Kenneth Paul Tan (2008), "Meritocracy and elitism in a global city: ideological shifts in Singapore", *International Political Science Review*, 29(1), 7–27.

13 Richard Stubbs (2009), "What ever happened to the East Asian Developmental State? The unfolding debate", *The Pacific Review*, 22(1), 1–22.

This is clearly a complex and dynamic situation that escapes a simple description of Singapore as an authoritarian state, or even as a political society that has been liberalising in a linear direction. Therefore, reductively technical accounts of Singapore's policy-making practice, ignoring the historical and political complexities within which this practice is embedded, will not have much pedagogical value. When these historical and political complexities are taken into account, however, Singapore does not seem like such a uniquely authoritarian model that has no relevance to other developing and advanced countries. Instead, the policy challenges that confront a de-caricatured Singapore present numerous instructive resonances with the experiences of other countries — resonances from which profound lessons may be drawn.

The LKY School: Research and Engagement

The LKY School needs to be understood in terms of this complex and evolving political environment. Only in its eighth year, the School is the newest participant in the collective process of codifying a Singapore approach to policy-making, but the first to systematically invite full international cohorts of Master degree students to engage critically with Singapore's experience of policy-making and governance. Bringing together in one historically iconic campus a thoroughly multinational community of faculty members and students with backgrounds in a range of academic disciplines and professional careers, the School is also well placed to intervene critically and constructively in the practice of policy-making in Singapore, not only by holding up a mirror to this practice, but also by bringing to the table multiple perspectives and the latest analytical approaches and tools. In the light of the "active citizenry" ideal espoused by the prime minister, it is not too much of a stretch to imagine a role for the School as a "corporate citizen" with a responsibility for participating in discussions and debates on matters of public importance.

Faculty members, often in their own professional capacities and sometimes on a *pro bono* basis, have engaged in consultancy work for ministries and agencies of the Singapore government as well as organisations in civil society. Many have been principal investigators in research projects funded or commissioned by the government. Many have also served on national committees and advisory councils, often as expert resource persons. Through its numerous custom-designed Executive Education programmes (often including "Singapore experience" components), the School has also provided training to not only governments and high-level delegations from countries that include Brunei, China, India, Kazakhstan, Mongolia, Taiwan, Vietnam and a number of African countries, but also officers serving in Singapore's public sector. Faculty members have real potential to be a positive influence on Singapore's public officers, not only by helping to sharpen their analytical tools and policy-making instruments, but — more importantly perhaps — by helping to prepare them for a different kind of citizenry whose needs and expectations are shaped by a different kind of political environment.

Another important area where the School has made a contribution to the codification of Singapore's policy practice is research and publications. Over the years, faculty members have published numerous peer-reviewed articles, books and book chapters, as well as presented papers at conferences and workshops on subjects that have direct relevance to policy-making in Singapore. One example is former IMF economist Henri Ghesquiere's *Singapore's Success: Engineering Economic Growth*, an illustrative case history that focuses on the workings of the Singapore economy, identifying the factors and decisions that have contributed cohesively to its successful growth and development.[14] Professor Neo Boon Siong's *Dynamic Governance: Embedding Culture, Capabilities and Change in Singapore*, an exhaustive volume, offers illustrative case studies and interview data to build up a governance framework based on the importance of "thinking ahead, thinking again, and thinking across".[15] Some economists at the School — including Visiting Associate Professor Ashish Lall, Professor Chen Kang, Associate Professor Gu Qingyang, Associate Professor Hui Weng Tat, Professor Mukul Asher, Visiting Professor Ramkishen Rajan, Associate Professor Tan Khee Giap and Assistant Professor Wong Marn Heong — have also been publishing work on a wide range of Singapore-relevant subjects including employment (local and foreign labour, skills

---

14 Henri Ghesquire (2007), *Singapore's Success: Engineering Economic Growth* (Singapore: Thomson Learning).

15 Neo Boon Siong (2007), *Dynamic Governance: Embedding Culture, Capabilities and Change in Singapore* (Singapore: World Scientific).

development, *etc.*), wages (inequalities, minimum wage, *etc.*), competitiveness, productivity, social security, investment, growth, crisis, equity and sustainability in Singapore. The School and Singapore's Ministry of Education also jointly produced a book, *Economics in Public Policies: The Singapore Story*, which has served as both a textbook for undergraduate and "A" level economics students as well as a reference book for policy-makers.[16] There have also been a large number of publications on social policy by Visiting Professor M. Ramesh, health care and public health policies by Associate Professor Phua Kai Hong, transport policies by Adjunct Professor Paul Barter and ethnic management policies by Dr. Suzaina Kadir. Some of this research is disseminated further when faculty members write opinion-editorials in the mainstream press and blog about their work online. Faculty members also appear regularly in the local and international media to provide expert comments on various Singapore-related issues.

My own research strongly features publications on Singapore, approached critically, sometimes unconventionally, and mainly through an inter-disciplinary combination of political science and cultural studies methodologies. I have been interested in exploring questions of governance, subjecting the practice of meritocracy and pragmatism, for instance, to critical analysis alongside related concerns about democracy and civil society. In my work on Singapore's creative city policies, I have explored the political, economic and cultural contexts of its arts and culture industry practices, highlighting cinema, television and theatre. I have also worked on topics related to the politics and public management of race, gender, sexuality, class and citizenship status in Singapore.

Encouraging more Singapore policy research would seem a sensible strategy for a global-minded public policy school in Asia. Indeed, from "off-the-record, one-on-one conversations" conducted with nearly all faculty members in 2011, then Vice-Dean Scott Fritzen noted that some faculty felt it was a "no-brainer" to base the School's distinctiveness on Asia-focused research. Some faculty, he explained, also believed that the School should explicitly encourage its faculty members to "engage critically on Singaporean public policy issues". However, there has always

---

16 Tan Say Sin, *et al.* (2009), *Economics in Public Policies: The Singapore Story* (Singapore: Marshall Cavendish).

been some reservation about how much of this research profile should be strongly Singapore-centred. Partly, as Fritzen also noticed, some faculty members expressed concerns that it would be "artificial" to feature research on Asia in its output. Partly, too, this reservation may arise from the incentive to "think big" in research, which has the effect of discouraging in-depth study of more narrowly formulated research questions, including those Singapore-centric areas that may on the surface seem overly parochial.

My own view is that research on Singapore need not be — and usually is not — inward-looking and disengaged from international discourses on public policy and governance. Much of the Singapore policy experience does not appear as an outlier when thinking about matters that concern the international community of academics and practitioners. Instead, this policy experience ranges from being a rich source of ideas in policy experimentation and implementation, to being a direct challenge to international orthodoxies associated mostly with liberal democratic thought and practice.

Engaging the Singapore experience with critical imagination and openness, and without any need for self-orientalist and occidentalist strategies, allows for a creative disruption of the continuities and inertia sustained by the hegemonic power of American social science, for instance, whose dominance and pretentions to universalism have been ensconced in the practice and standards of so-called "tier-one" journals so admired even by institutions located within economic, social and political contexts whose realities require a radically different critical approach. This, in effect, points to a central tension in the kinds of choices that faculty members, particularly younger members on tenure track, have to make in negotiating their careers: The dilemma of publishing in these journals versus doing locally impactful work often appears much too stark. One positive outcome of this tension at the LKY School has been the production of new high quality textbooks authored by its faculty members with the express aim of presenting policy knowledge that is beyond the particular realities of the North American world.[17]

---

17 For instance, Wu Xun, M. Ramesh, Michael Howlett and Scott Fritzen (2010), *The Public Policy Primer: Managing the Policy Process* (Routledge).

Given the more traditional demands of research, teaching and service that are integral to the professorial vocation, the LKY School will not be able to focus as directly and wholeheartedly on the Singapore experience of policy-making and governance, at least not in the ways that a dedicated body like the Civil Service College, for example, can. Nevertheless, the School does currently have four research centres. Two, in particular, do Singapore-centred research. The Asia Competitiveness Institute, whose aim is "to provide policy-relevant analysis on competitiveness in Singapore and the ASEAN region", has published a number of case studies and working papers on Singapore, as well as a report in 2009 on Singapore's competitiveness that submitted for the government's consideration several strong recommendations that included beefing up trade and investment ties with ASEAN countries and defining a Singapore-specific model of an "innovation-driven economy".[18] The Institute of Policy Studies (IPS) has brought a multidisciplinary approach and strategic thinking to its research on Singapore-centric subjects, helping policy-makers to understand and appreciate the changing attitudes and needs of Singaporeans. Its research profile includes areas like the arts, culture and media; demography and family; economics and business; politics and governance; and society and identity. Since 2000, IPS has been organising the annual Singapore Perspectives conference, which brings Singaporeans together to debate public policy challenges. Since 2003, it has been organising the biannual Singapore Economic Roundtable where select groups of Singaporeans come together to discuss major macroeconomic issues facing the country. The proceedings of both the Singapore Perspectives conference and Singapore Economic Roundtable are published.

The School has also been able to engage with the policy-making and political establishment through its system of adjunct professors and fellows. On this list have been former Singapore government ministers Aline Wong, Yeo Cheow Tong and George Yeo, as well as several former permanent secretaries including Peter Ho (also former Head of the Civil Service), James Koh Cher Siang, Ngiam Tong Dow (whose speeches and interviews have been collected and published), Lam Chuan Leong, Lim Siong Guan (also former Head of the Civil Service) and J.Y. Pillay (also

18 Christian Ketels, Ashish Lall and Neo Boon Siong (2009), *Singapore Competitiveness Report 2009* (Singapore: Lee Kuan Yew School of Public Policy).

responsible for turning Singapore Airlines into a successful global brand). Others on this list include Khoo Teng Chye, former chief executive of the Public Utilities Board; Lim Jim Koon, former editor of Singapore's flagship Chinese-language daily *Lianhe Zaobao*; and Liu Thai Ker, well-known architect and former chief planner of Singapore. Lee Kuan Yew himself is listed as a Distinguished Fellow of the School.

These adjunct professors bring much more than reputational value to the LKY School; their collective policy experience is a treasure trove. The challenge has been to find the most effective means of utilising it for the School's research, educational and policy outreach activities. Getting this right is still a work-in-progress, and the aim should be to generate healthy tensions and orchestrate productive collisions between the critical-theoretical strengths of the more academic faculty and the practical wisdom of policy professionals in order to create a vibrant policy space that avoids the excesses of formalistic abstraction as well as the idiocy of a vulgar and habitual form of pragmatism.

The LKY School's Educational Role

As an educator, I often think about what it is that the students really want out of their degree programme at the LKY School. I consider it important to understand this before being able to develop sound curriculum and pedagogical techniques that would suit their needs as learners. This does not mean treating students as customers and pandering to their demands. But it does mean taking their expectations seriously, before introducing new perspectives to them in ways that will add value.

In my mind, there are at least three types of students at the LKY School. First are the students who are strongly "vocational" in their outlook. They want to cut to the chase and get answers to problems that they recognise as important and urgent. They impatiently ask more "how to" than "why" questions. They see curriculum as a policy-making manual, the topics as policy tools and pedagogy as training. Second are students who are well-versed in their own traditional academic disciplines — such as economics, political science, law, business and so on — and they now want to bring their knowledge to bear on policy-making and management, perhaps with a view to careers in public service. This group of students tends to be younger than the first and, although they still have an eye on the vocational uses of their public policy education, they demonstrate more patience in engaging with materials and classroom activities that may not appear immediately useful. The third group of students, a minority at this stage, is mainly interested in understanding and advancing public policy and management as an academic discipline, focusing on its central assumptions, debates, methodological instruments and techniques, and even its historical development and future prospects.

Each of these expectations is, of course, entirely valid. The challenge for me — and I imagine for my colleagues as well — is to manage them in the classroom and to broaden each one to encompass an awareness of the value of the others. I try to excite the very practically-oriented students with the prospect of having theoretical lenses that can radically detach them from the day-to-day realities and labours of policy-making, give them alternative vision that can break the cognitive habits and impatience of a one-track mind, and help them imagine alternative possibilities that transcend the apparent inescapability of the present. I also try to excite the very academically-oriented students with demonstrations of how seemingly abstruse and archaic philosophies, theories and concepts are really embedded in many of the decisions and actions of policy-makers, even without their realising it. Through the use of case studies, for example, students can experience how ideas are commingled with reality and practice, and how both escape being completely subsumed by the other.

Students tell my colleagues and me that they would like to have more Singapore and Asian content in the curriculum. This is hardly surprising and entirely appropriate for a school whose primary mission is to educate and train the next generation of Asian policy-makers and leaders. The student body is made up not only of Singaporean students, or even Asian students. Over these eight years, students have come from more than 70 countries, representing every continent except Antarctica. A typical classroom at the LKY School mirrors a cosmopolis. Quite aside from the enormous learning potential that this diversity immediately sets up, the classroom can also serve as a platform for achieving greater global understanding and appreciation of Singapore. In soft power terms, the LKY School has the capacity to nurture leaders and future leaders who would be positively pre-disposed to Singapore.

Rather oddly, there has been a relatively low amount of Singapore content in the curriculum to date. Not one of the compulsory core modules is specifically about any aspect of Singapore, though they may use Singapore case studies for illustrative purposes. In the Master of Public Policy (MPP) core module "Politics and Public Policy", for instance, I designed different classroom activities for each week using a single case study of foreign domestic workers in Singapore to bring out different dimensions of the complex problem as seen through the ideological context (*e.g.* liberal capitalism, socialism, or feminism) discussed each week.

MPP students are all required to do a Policy Analysis Exercise (PAE), equivalent to a Master's dissertation, which often involves being attached to, or at least in communication with, government agencies and non-government organisations. Many of them tend to be based in Singapore. Students enrolled in the Master of Public Management (MPM) programme spend about six weeks on attachment to government agencies, mostly Singaporean ones.

Only 6 elective modules (the non-compulsory components of the curriculum) out of more than 80 are entirely on Singapore:

- Changes in Singapore's Political Economy
- Evolving Practices of Governance in Singapore
- Public Policy and Management in Singapore
- Singapore: The City
- Singapore's Development: A Comparative Analysis
- State-Society Relations in Singapore

A relatively small number of elective modules include some Singapore content, mainly in terms of using Singapore case studies or at least Singapore-based examples. The School has produced more than 30 Singapore case studies, mainly for teaching purposes, and plans to devote more resources and energy to expand this number. The current set of cases deal with topics in areas like law enforcement, public housing, public transport, urban redevelopment, education system, public health, social security, social services, population, ethnicity, water management, information and communications, foreign workers, foreign relations and foreign investment.

In "Singapore: The City", a module that I team-teach with Harvard Professor Alan Altshuler, a Singaporean view and an American view of Singapore's history of urban planning and development are deliberately juxtaposed in critical debate to foreground central concerns in the fields of political science and urban studies. We expanded the scope of learning by arranging visits to relevant government agencies and specific sites where tensions in urban planning decisions and implementation had to be negotiated and resolved. In this course, we both posed some very uncomfortable questions that forced not only the students but also ourselves as educators to confront the limits of our intellectual comfort zones.

"Evolving Practices of Governance in Singapore" is a module that I team-teach with former civil service chief Peter Ho. It is a critical exploration of the strengths and weaknesses of Singapore's practice of governance, couched in terms of public sector organisation, processes, outcomes, values, leadership and public participation. Students were given working knowledge of approaches and methods that the Singapore government has developed for understanding and managing risks and complexity. Working in teams, students were asked to imagine themselves to be a team of high-powered public officers drawn from various government agencies. Their task was to present a set of scenarios to the deputy prime minister based on well-defined focal concerns and driving forces.

In my module "State-Society Relations in Singapore", I assigned student teams the task of writing Singapore case studies with a range of suggested topics on which they were expected to conduct their own research. This was done during the first half of the semester when the class also focused on understanding the theoretical material. In the second half of the semester, the case studies were used as the basis for role-play scenarios that featured dilemmas and difficult decisions, carefully designed to raise problems that resulted from the collision of theory and practice. For public policy students, these role-play scenarios set up open-ended and somewhat realistic situations that allowed theory and concepts to be "experienced" and problematised. They were also an opportunity to practise or rehearse the kind of real-life activities not uncommon for political leaders and public managers. For example, one student team wrote a case on the public debate to legalise casinos in Singapore. I designed a role-play scenario in which some of the students imagined that they were corporate communications executives from different ministries and agencies tasked to brainstorm ideas for a comprehensive press statement to be issued by the Minister for Trade and Industry announcing the government's decision to go ahead with the integrated resorts proposal. They were also asked to draft talking points in anticipation of questions from the press and other stakeholders who could be present at the fictitious press conference, including representatives of various interests both supporting and opposing the casino decision.

An exercise like the above gets students to develop research and writing skills, to engage with the more conceptual material introduced in class, to frame the empirical data so that key learning points can be brought to the fore, and — in the role-play activity — to "experience" the dilemmas and challenges of working and negotiating with one another in a scenario that may serve as a rehearsal for real life. Students also come to better understand the evolving economic, social and political contexts of policy-making in Singapore, realising in particular that Singapore is not a simple caricature of an authoritarian state, but a complex political society whose policy experience is more widely resonant than they might have expected at first.

My emphasis on theory *and* practice at the LKY School comes out of a long-standing interest in developing praxial modes of learning, critically informed by theoretical reasoning and values. Before joining the LKY School, I had taught in the NUS Political Science department as well as the University Scholars Programme. During that time, I introduced and developed service learning in the form of semester-long attachments to civil society organisations. Designed to enable critical engagement with society, these attachments enriched classroom learning and let students experience for themselves how ideas, values, debates and contradictions played out in social and political life. Through classroom learning, students acquired different analytical lenses for making sense of a complex reality, learning how to make judgements and decisions within such complexity. This two-way process, which rarely happens without design, instantly transformed students into social agents and empowered them in profound and often unpredictable ways.[19]

---

19 Kenneth Paul Tan (2009), "Service learning outside the US: initial experiences in Singapore's higher education", *PS: Political Science and Politics*, 42(3), 549–557.

As I had a lot of experience in organising forums and seminars involving Singapore speakers on Singapore-related topics, I was in a good position to provide the strategic and academic directions and professional contacts for a co-curricular programme that would feature Singapore speakers and issues of interest to policy students and faculty at the LKY School. This would supplement the slowly growing Singapore content in the curriculum as well as the "Principles of Governance in Singapore" lecture that the Dean has been delivering to every cohort of students. Together with Elizabeth Quah, the Director of Strategic Planning at the time, we devised the entire programme called "The Singapore Experience@The LKY School".

The Bukit Timah Dialogue sessions were at the heart of the programme. These were fortnightly lunchtime seminars, about five to six each semester, which featured Singapore leaders in the public, private and non-profit sectors. They presented on a specific topic and then engaged in moderated discussion with the audience, normally consisting of between 30 to 80 participants. Immediately following a session, the speaker would adjourn for lunch with a group of about ten students (selected on a sign-up basis) to continue the discussion in a cosier setting. In planning the slate of speakers for each semester, much care was given to ensure that we presented a range of views, certainly not only those that were strongly pro-establishment. Over the years, speakers have included government ministers, permanent secretaries and senior civil servants, members of parliament, journalists, leaders in the business community, heads of charity and non-profit organisations, civil society activists and academics. Many of the themes reflected both the growing concerns and excitement of a Singapore whose policy-making practices were confronted with changing realities that required skilful adaptations, reinventions and transformations.

The Angsana Evenings — lively dialogues with eminent speakers presented in a "formal dinner" setting for about 50 participants — formed a second component of the Singapore Experience programme. We named these events after the large angsana tree that stands in the quadrangle in full view of the dining room. Guests have included filmmaker Tan Pin Pin who spoke about arts policy in Singapore, novelist Catherine Lim who gave a witty analysis of political liberalisation in Singapore, architect William Lim who presented on Singapore in the new world order, and Dana Lam, former president of feminist organisation AWARE, who screened her short film and shared her perspective on the AWARE saga. We also organised panels of speakers on themes such as Singapore's religious diversity and security policies.[20]

We called a third component of the Singapore Experience programme "Conversations". These were informal small group discussions with very senior figures in Singapore's public sector. The main idea was for the speakers to relate the circumstances surrounding a particularly difficult situation that they faced in their careers and how they dealt with it. The most effective sessions were very interactive in nature, with participants invited to explain what they would have done in such a situation.

In the fourth component of the Singapore Experience programme, we organised visits to key institutions, organisations and other places of interest. These have included trips to the Singapore Parliament, the Land Transport Authority Academy, the Urban Redevelopment Authority, the Marina Barrage, one of the Institutes of Technical Education, various heritage sites, the Sungei Buloh Wetland Reserve and various military open house events. Most were specially designed for our students and offered a chance for them to engage with senior policy-makers, organisation heads and civil society leaders. We even took students to the National Day Parade and a concert by the Singapore Symphony Orchestra held at the Esplanade. These trips were an effective way to get students to appreciate firsthand the broader society that forms the context of policy-making practices that they learnt about on campus. As far as possible, we tried to prepare materials that would maximise the learning points for students. To prepare students for the concert, for example, I gave a pre-concert lecture on arts policy in Singapore and Mahler's Tenth Symphony, which was the feature of that evening's programme.

We added a fifth component: a Singapore film club, featuring local films that I screened and followed with a discussion of what they could add to our under-standing of Singapore. In one of these sessions, filmmaker Eng Yee Peng was invited to screen her documentary films *Diminishing Memories I* and *II*, and to engage with

---

20   Both the Bukit Timah Dialogue sessions and the Angsana Evening talks have been video-recorded and DVDs are available for faculty and students to view and use for research and teaching.

the audience in a discussion of her feelings towards urbanization and the resettlement of Singapore's farming communities.

The Balance Between Engagement and Critical Distance

For an academic institution, bearing the name Lee Kuan Yew can be both a blessing and a challenge. It is a blessing because the association gives the School clout and attracts the support of many staunch admirers of the former prime minister, both in and out of Singapore. This, of course, makes the job of fundraising much less onerous and it must be one of the main reasons why the School could grow so rapidly in such a short period of time. However, it can be a challenge when members of the international academic community assume immediately that the School must be a propagator of Lee's ideas in ways that suggest the absence of academic freedom and complicity with what they regard as Singapore's lacklustre human rights record. This could have negative implications on the School's ability to form advantageous partnerships with overseas institutions and on its hiring strategies. This has not been a problem so far, though the perception of limits to academic freedom continues to linger uncomfortably.

There are many valid and necessary criticisms to be made of Singapore's political system and practice. I believe it is a duty particularly of the Singapore academic to cast a critical eye on the economy, society, culture and politics. This can be done from a basic position of loyalty to Singapore. Indeed, critical thinking has shaped my own writings and teaching.

In order to be vital and credible, academics at the LKY School should continue to deepen engagement with Singapore's policy-making establishment. But the School also needs to retain critical distance so that its faculty members can continue to see clearly enough to contribute alternative views and constructive criticism that policy-makers and political leaders may not like to hear, but need to. In a way, the LKY School must continue to be a responsible and active participant in helping to shape the ongoing social and political transformation in Singapore, while continuing to help codify a "Singapore School" of policy-making that will work well into the future.

Conclusion
Lessons Learned and the Road Ahead

Scott A. Fritzen

The broader significance of the Lee Kuan Yew School of Public Policy's first eight years does not lie in any particular set of achievements — substantial though these are. It lies in what this experience implies about the changing world of public policy education and about the unfinished enterprise of "building a global policy school in Asia". In this final chapter, we look outwards, towards the field of policy education; and forwards, towards some of the unanswered questions the school — and others in its mould — will continue to struggle with in the years to come.

Looking Outwards: Public Policy Education Goes Global

Scholarly research in universities like NUS centres on faculty talking mainly among themselves — carrying on highly technical discussions and debates in publications that are refereed by peers, and that ultimately aim at understanding the world better in some way.

Policy education, in contrast, has always centred on an ethos of *relevance to the world*, as a first-order priority. The point has been not merely to understand the world, but to serve it.

But "the world" has changed in decades since the field of public policy emerged in the middle of the 20th Century, in a host of ways that have implications for the field as a whole. To name but a few:

- *Increasing interdependence, complexity and systemic risk* mark virtually all areas of policy-making and governance, in virtually all settings: from economic integration to environmental sustainability. This should increase the demand for relevant policy analysis, while underscoring how difficult the curriculum challenge in policy education will be.

• In *an increasingly multi-polar world*, virtually all existing institutions for addressing common problems have come under stress. The increasing importance of the study and development of global governance institutions is obvious.

• Contests over the appropriate *roles of states, societies and markets* have resurfaced with a vengeance across the world. Policy schools need to rethink and reorient their sometimes government-centric curriculum.

• *The pace of change is accelerating*, placing a premium on the capacity of individuals, organisations and systems to learn and adapt. In terms of scholarship, our understanding of even basic processes in human polities and economies is tracking a moving target.

Fundamentally, policy schools try to have an impact on the world in two ways: professional training and research. In both of these, the area of relevance has never been more important and never been easy. Against the trends noted above, the field of public policy is experiencing renewed stress. Some speak of policy education going through an "age of anxiety", due to a pervasive sense that the core of its traditional model — essentially, producing analysts who will staff core government bureaus — is no more than another niche market at present. Fifty years ago, at the high watermark of what has been described as "high modernism", one might have predicted a different trajectory, and a different destination, but the obvious fact is that there is no clear professional field for which the typical policy degree is unambiguously the most appropriate entry ticket.

As a result of these trends, the field has seen contradictory tendencies towards fragmentation and convergence. The number of offshoot degrees and specialisations has proliferated, even as the core curriculum of most policy schools has remained remarkably stable. The same is true for the emerging "global" schools, from Berlin to Beijing to Singapore; much is shared on the curriculum front, even as positioning, research orientation, student target groups and degree programme niches vary. Yet "stability in the core" does not necessarily bode well, given the broader "existential crisis" facing the field. Despite — or perhaps because — public policy is a "sunrise industry", to quote Kishore Mahbubani, the need for innovative approaches has never been greater. Such approaches will inevitably need to go beyond tinkering with electives and specialisations. They will need to challenge some fundamental assumptions about what truly relevant policy education and scholarship look like.

As the number of the schools with an explicitly global orientation grows, the opportunities for these schools to engage with each other and with longer-established schools will increase. While a number of schools will maintain their primarily domestic orientation, global public policy education is likely to be a vibrant space for promoting relevance in the policy education enterprise.

Looking Back, Looking Ahead: Lessons and Unanswered Questions

What can we say about the road ahead for the LKY School? Martin Heidegger once spoke of the very existence of man taking the form of a question — and the same might be said of the existence of a global policy school in Asia. From a close reading of the chapters in this volume — each with its own voice, each touching the proverbial elephant from a different direction — comes a series of questions that will continue to shape the future of the School. Here are three.

What does it take to launch a global policy school? "Global policy school" here could mean many things (see Appendix A for a full treatment), but at a minimum it signals an intention:

- to benchmark oneself against some of the most prominent policy schools in the world; and
- to have an orientation and, eventually, an impact that is global in its scope.

Given how amorphous the concept of global policy still is, it may seem foolish to offer any clear roadmap for success. But for the sake of stimulating discussion, we can tease out several factors that have surfaced throughout this volume and that collectively seem to have gone into the equation — for the LKY School at least.

Two key factors emphasised by Kishore Mahbubani are significant resources and a stable, enabling environment — the existence of powerful stakeholders who wish the experiment to be successful. One cannot exaggerate the importance of these basic parameters of finance and support; lack one or both, and there is little chance of achieving critical scale.

Another key element is positioning. The rapid rise of the LKY School clearly has much to do with its location and to timing. Singapore is a cosmopolitan, vibrant city-state with an outsized reputation for excellence in public administration. It lies in the middle of the world's fastest growing and integrating region. And this region is a veritable laboratory of different governance arrangements — in an age in which everyone agrees that governance plays a decisive role in determining development outcomes. There are many different niches a global policy school might occupy, but this one is close to being ideal.

Deft leadership at the LKY School level has played a role as well. Though impossible to quantify, the effect of the driving ambition and extensive personal and professional networks of a founding dean such as Kishore Mahbubani is formidable.

In short, the successful launch of the LKY School as a global policy school (call it *GPS Launch*) can be described as a function of resources, support, positioning and leadership, or:

$$Strong\ GPS\ Launch = R + S + P + L$$

The question of what factors might be needed to *sustain* a strong launch is an interesting one. The above elements above must themselves be sustained, but different factors may play an increasingly important role as well. Growing an academic culture and broadening the leadership team — issues discussed in Chapter 3 — undoubtedly become more critical with each passing year. In their absence, the gap between external perception and expectations of the School, and its substantive performance and quality, could become untenable. And it is fair and realistic to note that there have been several times in recent years when the leadership team and faculty of the LKY School have asked ourselves, uncomfortably, whether in practice we merited the sky-rocketing reputation and external visibility the School had achieved. Indeed, the question has to some extent fuelled our determination to pursue internal reforms, to *not* become complacent.

The question of sustainability is in fact currently coming again into focus for the School's leadership. Faculty and leadership team turnover in mid-2012 is at an all-time high. The School's entrepreneurial growth phase arguably placed significant strain on its staff. Partly as a result, administrative staff morale has at times been surprisingly low, as assessed at least by two rounds of an organisational health survey conducted for the School *pro bono* by McKinsey & Company. It has taken the School longer to build up predictable management processes and to nurture an academic culture than it has to grow the enterprise structurally. The question of sustainability is necessarily still open — not least because the second of our "unanswered questions" is still open, namely:

How will we know success when we see it? Launching a global policy school implies a destination. But it can be surprisingly difficult to get agreement among key stakeholders on how to mark whether or not we are on track — to programme the Global Positioning System for the Global Policy School, so to speak. From its inception, the School's leadership and key stakeholders looked (with the help of the McKinsey study described in Chapter 2) systematically at outside models and benchmarks, and tried to be deliberative in laying out a roadmap for the (primarily structural) growth of the School.

But after struggling with the issue for years, Kishore Mahbubani's point that "there is no gold standard" in public policy education is obvious to most of us. This implies that alongside the need for strategic blueprints, there is also a need to be adaptive and creative. Executive education, research promotion and the "Singapore/ Asia" question are all examples where the need to strike this balance surfaced throughout this volume.

Stavros Yiannouka in Chapter 2 tells the story of how, within a few years, the executive education enterprise of the LKY School has become one of the largest in the world (for a policy school). How should we measure success in this endeavour? A truthful answer is that there is no clear "bottom-line" metric to answer this question. The obvious indicators for a private sector enterprise — size, growth, profit — are important but insufficient to capture the impact of the programmes. The quality of the constituent programmes is difficult to assess; programme impact, even more so. In the LKY School as elsewhere, efforts to assess programme quality and impact in executive education rarely go beyond simple participant feedback exercises. Meanwhile, many policy schools carry on quite well without executive education altogether. And uneasy questions about the appropriate scale of executive education (relative to degree programmes) and relevant geographic coverage of programmes have also been raised intermittently over the years, particularly as the transaction costs of mounting programmes in relatively far-flung locations (such as Central Asia) have increased.

At the same time, there is in fact good reason to believe executive education has been an important driver of the School's impact through professional education. Executive education at the LKY School is showing incipient synergies with the degree programmes (for instance, original case studies developed by faculty and associated researchers at the School find use in both degree and executive programme classrooms), and the range of original programming, and the high profile of the participants, are impressive. The point here is that there is no external model to be copied in answering difficult questions about the right scale and focus of executive education at the School. Here as in the other areas below, we should be willing to adopt and adapt best practices where they exist elsewhere, but we should not be surprised if we find a real need to innovate in order to take the state of our game to the next level.

Research promotion is another good example. There is no shortage of indicators with which to measure progress and benchmark the School's output against competitors. There is only one regrettable problem. These indicators are all highly flawed. At a minimum, they are incomplete, particularly in the context of a policy school, as Astrid Tuminez points out in Chapter 4; it takes a fairly heroic and sustained managerial effort for any of these indicators *not* to be misused or misleading (at least in isolation). A fatal mistake a policy school can make in this setting is to pretend it is simply "another academic discipline" — a department of politics or economics, with research to be assessed in more or less the same way as in those departments. And this mistake is very easy to make in an ambitious global research university like NUS, because that will be the comfortable "fall back" answer in the absence of a proactive definition of research impact and "value-add" in global policy schools.

There is an even greater mistake to avoid: that is, to do exactly the opposite and to neglect to develop a robust dialogue and accountability system around research issues. And in truth, a number of emerging policy schools are very much in danger of making this mistake as well. Between these two extremes lies a "middle path". There is no single dominant indicator in the middle path; quantitative indicators are employed in combination with other methods — such as direct assessment of the quality of a research portfolio — to develop a robust dialogue, culture and accountability system around research issues. And the system that emerges is one that must serve the special context and mission of a global policy school. To say this is easy. But again, there is no "gold standard" in research benchmarking for a professional policy school, nothing that can be bought off-the-shelf.

A final example of the need to define success iteratively and imaginatively relates to the theme of connecting the School to the Singaporean environment. Developing a motif found in every chapter, Kenneth Paul Tan in Chapter 5 sketched out a remarkably difficult set of questions, both conceptual and practical, that the existence of a global policy school in Singapore has surfaced, with the fundamental question on how to leverage Singapore as a policy laboratory *par excellence*, without losing a constructive, critical "distance" from the subject. This distance would allow multiple voices rather than a single narrative of "the Singapore story" to come to the fore; and it would highlight the critical question of the *transferability* of Singaporean lessons to the diverse country contexts from which our students and executive education participants hail. This process of more proactive engagement with Singaporean themes has begun in the School. In this and other areas, the answers are best "cooked" slowly and thoughtfully. Once again, we conclude there is no particular cookbook outlining how to do this for an emerging school in an emerging field.

Who owns the Lee Kuan Yew School of Public Policy? We return to one of the first questions posed in this volume. Obviously, many individuals and collectivities have shaped and continue to shape the trajectory of the School. External constituencies include key individuals within the Singaporean establishment, the School's Governing Board, the NUS leadership team and perhaps some influential network partners such as the Harvard Kennedy School. Internal constituencies include, of course, the faculty, staff and students of the School. All lay legitimate claims on the LKY School's mission and strategy, yet all have somewhat different interests and biases.

As difficult as answering it may be, this is a question that cannot remain rhetorical; a continuous stream of decision points confronts the School's management team, and standing still is not an option. But any given answer never "stands" for long. How will external and internal stakeholders engage over the future of the School? Much will depend in large measure on the Dean's leadership. Yet while it is true that deans stand at the intersection of the internal and external stakeholders of any school, and that the LKY School Dean in particular enjoys considerable autonomy under its Charter, the pattern of engagement contains many wild cards. How the stakeholders will interrelate on a host of issues — from making senior appointments (including the eventual transition from a founding to a second Dean for the School) to validating the performance of the School — is more like a complex dance than a narrow script.

An even more complex dance relates to the balance between the core management team and the academic culture in the School. As Stavros Yiannouka outlined in Chapter 2, the School's management has been both centralised and entrepreneurial. There is little doubt that, as the faculty matures, a greater space for faculty self-governance and more predictable management processes must be carved out.

The dance goes on.

* * *

"There is no safe harbour. We must build and repair the ship on the open seas. *There is no safe harbour.*"

The former president of NUS, Professor Shih Choon Fong, was fond of this phrase. Certainly, he was a master builder of ships on the open seas: Under the able leadership of his team, including current President Tan Chorh Chuan, the international reputation, faculty scholarship, student recruitment and curricula of NUS all turned decisively towards world-class status.

In a farewell appreciation dinner held for him in November 2008, President Shih used a different metaphor. NUS, he said, was like a rocket successfully launched and soaring through the atmosphere, "fuelled in large part by our embrace of global excellence" — but still not free of the earth's gravitational pull.

Many tensions have been described throughout this book and this concluding chapter, among others:

- between internal and external stakeholders shaping the School;
- between learning from competitors and forging one's own path;
- between entrepreneurial management and faculty empowerment; and
- between a "global" vision and *clientele* and "Singaporean" roots.

They represent a fuel for creative institution building; they will, after all, never be resolved definitively. Learning from President Shih, any failure to engage these tensions would surely represent "the familiar forces of gravity and atmospheric resistance" pulling the School off course.

Achieving "lift-off" has not been easy, and sustaining early momentum in institution building will be even more difficult, whether for NUS or for the Lee Kuan Yew School of Public Policy.

But as the School soon completes its first decade of existence, there is no doubt that the sights of the School's faculty, administrators, alumni, students and partners are firmly trained skywards.

Global Public Policy as a Field of Study: A View from Asia

Kanti Bajpai, Scott A. Fritzen, and Kishore Mahbubani[1]

This paper addresses three questions (as posed in Robert Lieberman's paper):[2]

- How is global public policy (GPP) distinctive as a field of study?
- What can globally focused schools of public policy offer a troubled world?
- How can the global public policy network (GPPN) help the field of global public policy grow and be better recognised?

We suggest that GPP as a field of study is distinct from its "feeder" disciplines of economics, political science, and management studies: (i) in the degree to which it is concerned with government policy-making towards the common good both at the global and domestic levels; (ii) in its multi disciplinary nature; and (iii) in its focus on training public servants. It is vocational in this third sense. It is more than vocational though in the sense that its research ambitions and protocols are (or should be) no less than those of the other social sciences.

GPP programmes, we suggest, will vary given differing histories and social, economic, political, and geopolitical contexts and have much to offer a globalising world by way both of training, research, and policy consultancy. Finally, we note that GPPN is a useful forum for discussing evolving best practices at a time of global change and should continue to foster student exchange and faculty collaboration and

---

1   The authors would like to thank Benjamin Shatil, Darryl Jarvis, Eduardo Araral and Ora-orn Poocharoen from the LKY School for their comments on an earlier draft of this paper presented at the GPPN Conference, Rockefeller Foundation, Bellagio, Italy, 14–18 June 2011.

2   Robert C. Lieberman, "The Future of Global Public Policy Education", paper presented at the Conference on the Future of Global Public Policy Education, Rockefeller Foundation, Bellagio, Italy, 14–18 June 2011.

exchange. As GPP proliferates as a field of study, which it looks set to do, the field may be invigorated by the relative newcomers.

GPP as a Field of Study

Drawing boundaries around an intellectual field is always fraught with difficulty since the natural and social world is seamless and phenomena are interconnected. Yet boundaries are more or less tightly or loosely drawn, at least as a convenience. What follows recognises the difficulty of bounding as also the inescapable drive to partition reality and the world of academic teaching and research.

GPP as a field bears the marks of its precursors and feeder disciplines. At the same time, it has evolved a character of its own. The distinctness of public policy studies — and by "studies" we mean here both the teaching and research programme — is not surprisingly therefore more a matter of degree. We should clarify here to that throughout the paper when we address the question "What is policy studies or GPP?" we understand that the answer is and always has been plural — programmes have differed in their conception of what it is to do public policy studies. Any attempt to represent the field therefore risks a certain amount of caricature, and we plead guilty to that charge.

Also, we understand that any description of what public policy studies or GPP has to deal with two interconnected but not always related depictions — what the aspiration of the field is as depicted in influential writings on the field and in its advertising brochures; and what the field is in terms of its teaching and research: what we say we want the field to be and what we advertise it as being (to clients) may well differ from what the actual experience of the field is. With these prefatory thoughts, we attempt an answer to the question of what public policy studies and GPP are. We will assert a number of things rather baldly and then problematise them in what follows.

GPP is an outgrowth of public policy studies, and so it is useful to begin with a picture of the public policy field. Public policy in turn has grown out of the feeder disciplines of economics, political science, and management studies but seems to be distinct from them in three ways: it is focused on what governments should and actually do for the public good; it is multi-disciplinary; and it is aimed primarily at training those interested in public service and, through its teaching and research, in the improvement of government. Global public policy is distinct from its older cousin, public policy, in its attempt to identify connections and study tensions between domestic policy-making and global public goods.

Public Policy Studies as What Governments Do for the Public Good

Public policy studies as a field is about what governments can or should do for the common good. This statement foregrounds two things. The first is the centrality of governments in making policies for the common good. The second is the insistence on the common good as being the objective of government endeavour. Clearly, there are other social actors that work for the common good or at least aspire to do so. Clearly, also, not everything governments do are for the public good. Government agents do things for their own personal (or group) benefit or the benefit of their political masters, and public policy-making is often plagued by extreme fragmentation and mutually debilitating rather than synergistic actions across agencies and levels of government: venality and pathology can therefore make governments dysfunctional in terms of the common good.

Still, it is our contention that the *starting point* for public policy studies is the notion that governments are the most important agents of policies towards the common good and that the common good is a central aim of government functioning. In today's world and for the foreseeable future, it is difficult to see any social actor replacing government as the main agent of the common good. A charismatic individual or various actors in civil society may seek to define the common good, but in the end it is the organization called government above all that must give policy expression to the definition and to implement it. The notion of the common good will vary in time and space (and is itself the object of debate and research), but the idea that governments do and must have a conception of it and that governments will be the primary agents of its attainment, even if influenced by a variety of non-governmental actors, at home and abroad, must be at the heart of public policy studies. At the very least, we must begin with the assumption that government is about the pursuit of the common good.

Since other social actors help define the common good and often aid or impede the government in implementing policies and since, as noted earlier, functionaries and departments of the government itself can be dysfunctional in policy-making, the study of these other actors is also part of public policy studies if only because though they rarely supplant government, they can be powerful influences on the functioning of government. We would maintain though that in saying this we have not significantly diluted the proposition that public policy studies is primarily about government functioning towards the common good.

Are public policy programmes unique in studying government policies towards the common good? Economics does bear upon government policies, but it is not focused exclusively or even primarily upon government. Political science as a field certainly concerns itself with government, far more so than economics, but its canvas is much larger than governments and the common good. The interests and roles of individuals, ethnic communities, sectional groups (classes, associations, businesses), international and transnational organizations in shaping social reality is much more important for political studies as compared to public policy studies.

Does this make public policy completely distinct from those disciplines? No, but the greater emphasis on government actions towards the public good in public policy programmes is, we would suggest, distinctive enough to warrant a special field of teaching and research. The separation of fields is historically constituted and not intrinsic. Economics, political science, and philosophy were once deeply integrated in a common field of speculation and study. Their separation was a sociological process, at least in part a convenience as knowledge expanded to the point where few if any scholars could claim intellectual command over the totality of information and ideas in it. As the role of governments has grown in social life, so a field dedicated to the study of government policy was created and has evolved.

Public Policy Studies are Multi-Disciplinary

Public policy programmes are distinct in being more multi-disciplinary than their feeder disciplines. Public policy programmes are primarily built around courses in economics (micro- and macro-economics, international trade, development, public regulation, statistics, modelling, *etc.*), political science (public policy studies consisting of public administration, policy formulation and implementation, policy evaluation and analysis, *etc.*), and management studies (budgeting, public services delivery, organizational systems and processes in government and the public sector, executive leadership, *etc.*).

Courses in these areas obviously address different dimensions of what governments do. They are not altogether integrated (or *inter*-disciplinary) because of the formidable conceptual and theoretical differences (at the very least) between these disciplines and because few faculty possess knowledge of all three. But the quest to press all three disciplines (and beyond) into the service of *practical problem-solving for the public good* is an important guiding ideal in professional policy education.

Here again, while public policy is different from economics, political science, and management studies, we should not exaggerate the difference. Economics and political science in particular do not usually feature courses from other disciplines and do not hire PhDs from other fields, yet the purity of these fields is largely a myth. For instance, doctoral students in economics and perhaps more so political science have for some time now been encouraged to study — or have sought out — a secondary field of study in another social science. Academic writings in economics, political science, and the other social sciences draw on the insights of other fields and often cut across disciplines. Within economics and political science, there is considerable variety and some degree of incommensurability. A doctoral programme in, say, political science in the US includes sub-fields as diverse as American government and politics, comparative politics, international relations, political economy, political theory, and public policy. Students in these disparate sub-fields often can scarcely comprehend each other, differing as they do over theory, method, and the central questions and puzzles.

Public Policy Studies are for Public Servants

Public policy programmes are distinct in being primarily — though not exclusively — aimed at training public servants. Teaching and research on what governments do or should do is useful not just for those who are already in public service or aspire to be but also for the larger public — the citizenry — who might want information and ideas about what their or other governments do. Yet we contend that the most important function of public policy programmes has been training the serving and aspiring administrator as well as the "policy entrepreneur" seeking to influence societal change in a particular direction. The curriculum attempts to better equip those already in public service or those who wish to enter public service (whether in the public or non-profit sectors) to serve the common weal through a programme of reading, debate, and research. The research output of public policy faculty aims to improve the policy skills of practitioners (how to make and implement policy) and their substantive knowledge of policy fields. In this sense, public policy studies are vocational.

It is probably fair to say that economics, political science, and less so management studies, as programmes of study, are not primarily interested in training serving or putative civil servants. Graduate programmes in these fields are dedicated to producing the next generation of faculty who will dedicate themselves to research agendas driven by fairly well-established paradigms and puzzles. While this is so, clearly many public servants will be graduates of economics and political science in particular and will use what they have learned in larger or lesser measure in their jobs. Also, many economists and political scientists are interested in disseminating their research findings to governments. Once again, we note a difference between public policy as a field and cognate social sciences, but we insist on not exaggerating the difference.

Public Policy and "Global Public Policy"

Global public policy (GPP) is distinct from its older cousin in its globalness. Public policy programmes are increasingly global or international, at least in their aspirations. There is recognition in public policy schools, and particularly in the four schools in GPPN, that the curriculum and research ambit, students, and faculty must be more international than ever before.

Public policy schools are more global in terms of the curricular topics covered, the readings and sources that are assigned, and in the cases examined and examples cited. This is likely to grow, partly as scholarship in public policy expands (which in turn is a function of the proliferation of public policy programmes and the attraction of scholars from all over the world to them). Research areas are more global too. For the first time, the Western and, more specifically, US experience is no longer necessarily the gold standard. Public policy research is beginning to examine the experiences and practices of other societies and learn lessons from them. The experiences and practices of countries which have been successful in economic transformation — many of which are in Asia — are coming to be regarded as highly instructive for other countries in the global South and beyond.

Curriculum and research are more global also in the sense that issues of the global commons and global public goods are increasingly of moment: natural disasters, climate change, deadly diseases, the world economy, international finance and banking, proliferation, and terrorism (amongst other problems) are all challenges which are profoundly cross-national in their origins and in the coordination challenge they pose to countries seeking to manage them.

There is another key sense in which GPP is different from older public policy studies in terms of the degree of globalness. This arises from globalisation. Technology is interconnecting individuals, communities, groups, and countries as never before. The actions of distant peoples and societies can have unintended as well as intended effects — and with unprecedented speed and consequence. Policy-making, even for the national common good, cannot be separated easily from sectional and other national interests far away. Increasingly, norms and standards are being defined by a melange of actors (including governments and international and transnational organisations) operating around issue nodes and networks. Government policies are being made in a context that is defined by these norms and standards. GPP programmes must inevitably therefore pay much greater attention to these nodes and networks — what they are, how they came to be, how they operate, and what impact they have on governments.

Public policy programmes are also more global in terms of the internationalisation of the student body. Economic growth in Asia, Africa, and Latin America has meant that there are many more students from these areas who can pay for a public policy degree and who are willing to go abroad to get it. Governments in the developing countries have been more willing to pay for civil servants to improve their skills through relatively short programmes of advanced study in public policy. Knowledge of public policy as a field has increased with each succeeding generation that has gone to public policy schools and shared its experiences. Awareness has also grown as a function of internet access, which has spread the word about public policy programmes.

The internationalisation of the student body is not all demand driven. Public policy schools have been increasingly on the look-out for international students — partly for financial reasons and partly out of a sense that diversity matters in a globalised world. (Indeed, this trend is part and parcel of the "internationalisation" of higher education which is affecting universities across the world.)

Public policy faculty will also be more international in the years to come if they are not already so. As jobs have become hard to find in North America and Europe, as the rise of Asia has captured the imagination, and as Asian university salaries and infrastructure as well as living conditions have improved, faculty from all over the world that might otherwise have chosen North America and Europe will choose Asia. Africa and Latin America will also begin to attract international faculty. We note here that an increasing number of non-Western universities is appearing each year in the various rankings of the top 100 global research universities, and this will draw scholars from all over the world to them.

The "global" in GPP does not merely mean "more international" in a narrow sense, however. It also means questioning the assumptions of a field that has traditionally been rooted in domestic policy. How, for example can we explore ways in which domestic policies must adapt to create global public goods, or the effect that global public policies (as created by the UN/ICJ/WTO, *etc.*) have on domestic government policies. The intellectual terrain we cover is characterised by extensive interactions between levels in a governance system — from local to global — as well as between actors across the public-private-people sector divides. Global public policy must be fundamentally about elucidating and explaining interconnectedness and interaction effects, and ultimately about guiding effective action, within this "governance matrix".

While global public policy as an emerging field is more global than the field was, say, twenty years ago, we do not wish to suggest that there was nothing international about public policy in its earlier incarnations. It would be foolish to suggest that the great public policy schools that pioneered the field were impervious to the need for teaching, research, student intake, and faculty hiring that were "international". Indeed, several top policy schools — including Columbia SIPA and the Woodrow Wilson School of Public and International Affairs at Princeton — were founded with a strong international orientation and mission from the get-go.

Public Policy Studies and Other Social Sciences

Public policy as a field of study attracts a certain amount of skepticism — particularly from its feeder disciplines, economics, political science, and management studies — on at least three counts: for the absence of an "intellectual core", for being an "applied" field, and for lack of "rigour". Faculty from these disciplines claim that public policy studies' main distinction from these feeders lies in being an inferior product. We argue that GPP programmes should stop being apologetic in as much as the three criticisms could also be applied to the feeder disciplines.

Public policy studies have been looked down upon by both economics and political science (and to a negligible extent by management studies, which has been plagued by its own periodic identity crises) for the apparent absence of an intellectual core (*i.e.*, a coherent set of theories, methods, and problematics). This is somewhat surprising given that those disciplines are themselves quite divided on issues of theory, method, and the central questions and puzzles of their fields. Surely it is a deep caricature of economics and political science to suggest that they are unified, untroubled fields of intellectual endeavour. The battles within these disciplines are the stuff of legend. Nor is the problem of difference restricted to these social sciences. The same can easily be said of anthropology, psychology, and sociology, not to mention history and philosophy (if these are allowed into the domain of social science). The so-called "hard" or natural sciences fare little better in this regard, with fundamental and inflammatory divides between various schools and perspectives.

Public policy as a field of study has also been derided for being "applied", as if there were any fields of human inquiry that were so "pure" as not to bear on the practical life-world of human beings. Even very abstruse parts of mathematics relating to number theory have found application in everyday life. Certainly, to claim that economics and political science are not, at the end of the day, policy sciences would be indefensible.

A third criticism of public policy studies is that they are not rigorous, that the logics and empirics of a field are of questionable consistency: argumentation does not follow the strict rules of logic, statements derived from a set of primitive terms and assumptions do not inexorably or convincingly follow, and data gathering and processing are flawed (suffering from problems of validity, reliability, *etc.*). It is also suggested that hypotheses or research questions are not clearly stated, grounds for falsification and confirmation are not specified, and selection of cases are not properly justified. And so on. This criticism also is puzzling. Judging by the controversies in the various social and natural sciences (and we include here the applied sciences as well, such as engineering), there is no dearth of hand-wringing over precisely such issues in those fields. In saying this, we do not exculpate the field of public policy; but to suggest that, as a field, it is less rigorous than its cousins has not been systematically demonstrated and is a rather lazy conjecture. There is no reason in principle why public policy studies, informed by the older disciplines that it draws on, cannot aspire to greater rigour and match the best work in the older fields.

Our point therefore is that public policy is not all that different from the other social sciences and does not have to apologize for its existence. Its distinctiveness does not reside in its lack of coherent core, in its being an applied field, and in its supposed lack of rigour. Rather, its distinctiveness historically has arisen from a fairly resolute focus on what governments should and actually do for the public good, multi-disciplinarity, a commitment to training those interested in public service, and, through its research, a concern with improving government. Even here, the difference is one of degree, discernible enough to justify the separation of the programme but not so great as to suggest that public policy is a completely new and separate field.

Ultimately, the point is not whether or not GPP is a completely separate field, but that the growing awareness of "global" dimensions of policy, as defined earlier, is shaping institutional identities and discursive practices in ways that will improve the relevance of policy studies to the contemporary world. And that there is no going back.

What Can a GPP Programme Offer the World?

We suggest that GPP schools/programmes can offer the following:

- Training for public servants beyond civil service training academies
- Comparative perspectives on public policy
- Multi-disciplinary tools for public policy analysis
- Intellectual bridging skills for a complex, globalised, interconnected world
- Relating national interests to the global commons and global collective action
- Fostering epistemic communities amongst decision-makers
- Policy consultancy

Training Public Servants

GPP programmes fundamentally hold the promise of training those who will work in the public realm (including in international organizations), primarily putative and serving civil servants as well as those in the non-profit sector, but also including — and trending to an increasing degree — individuals targeting careers working in the public-private sector interface. Like all education, it aims to serve as a short-cut to learning. What might be learned through years of experience and trial and error by each generation of public servants may be distilled and transmitted in a short period of time. The training of those who will work in the public realm might be done by dedicated institutions run by governments, and clearly some of this is vital in order to produce a cohesive group with an *esprit de corps*. Not least in the developing world, however, government training capacity is limited, for a variety of reasons. The constraints include insufficient funding, the lack of expert trainers, and political interference in the curriculum. GPP programmes, run by academics, offer a way of overcoming these last two limits, but also the promise of a truly more global and comparative approach to policy education, one which arguably cannot be achieved by sitting in a classroom filled solely with members of one's own country's civil service.

Comparative Lessons

GPP is more comparative than its predecessors. The injection of the word "global" encourages scholars and students of public policy to look at the world around them and climb out of their national wells. In doing so, there are at least three lessons they might learn. The first is that their national policies are "better" than policies in other countries and do not need to be changed. This can be reassuring and reinforcing and is every bit as important as copycat policy-making. The second is that others have dealt with the issue in a more efficient and creative way, and there are elements that can be adapted. The third is that other countries are doing things that have not even entered the policy domain in their own country, and these might either be brought into the policy domain or are better left alone ("if it ain't broke, don't fix it"). Knowing when to leave well alone is a very important lesson, and comparative study can be helpful in learning negative lessons.

Multi-Disciplinarity

GPP provides a multi-disciplinary perspective on policy. It trains students to think about policy from various perspectives, primarily from the point of view of economics, political science, and management studies. The alleged weakness of public policy training, namely, that it is multi-disciplinary and risks being superficial, is its strength. GPP gives those who want to go on serving the public weal a chance to conceive of policy from several perspectives. Those who argue for narrow specialisation and intense knowledge of a field forget that there is always a need for those who can act as a bridge between narrow specialists and lofty generalists. GPP graduates are those potential bridges.

Bridging Skills in a Globalised World

This bridging skill is particularly important in a globalised world. GPP holds the promise of producing students who can make better sense of a complex interconnected world. In a globalised planet, where distant peoples, governments, and non-state actors are linked, this is a key skill. GPP students are akin to public intellectuals who can communicate intelligently, intelligibly, and incisively about complex matters to audiences that do not have the time or skills to comprehend the complicated world around them. GPP graduates are the public intellectuals of public service.

Connecting the National Interest and the Global Good

GPP gives students an opportunity to connect the national interest to the global interest, to understand how national welfare might be improved by global public goods, and to comprehend the difficulties of fashioning collective action even when it is clear that everyone benefits from a global compact. GPP training can help students identify the non-obvious, non-tautological reasons why collective action fails — and how and when it succeeds.

Fostering an Epistemic Community

GPP offers the possibility of producing what Peter Haas has called an "epistemic community" that could further the cause of international cooperation. Haas' argument is that international cooperation can be built by knowledge-based experts who are placed strategically in the policy making process and can, through a common pool of information, cause-and-effect logic, and normative commitments, guide their governments towards cooperative agreements. Haas' notion offers a way of thinking about the contributions of a GPP with a high complement of international students who either already are, or will be, in positions of decision-making authority. At the very least, GPP may produce a common or commensurate vocabulary for decision-makers working in different cultures and political systems.

Policy Consultancy for Governments and the World

A GPP school functions not only as a training school but also as a think tank for the global commons and national policies. Except for the US (and perhaps even in the US), there are not enough institutes dedicated to thinking about the global commons. In the developing world, by contrast, there are few institutions that can think systematically about national policies and fewer still that concern themselves with the global commons. GPP schools should offer their expertise to international organizations and perhaps even more so national governments. International and government civil servants face two key constraints — they must operate within policy orthodoxies and relatively short time horizons and therefore either will not or cannot do the kind of analytics that creative problem solving might require. The ability to step outside the standard frameworks of policy thinking and to do deeper, more rigorous, theoretically informed studies of a policy problem is the potential advantage of academic life and therefore of GPP schools. A GPP school must fulfil this "think-tank" role even as it functions as a teaching institution.

A Global Public Policy Curriculum

Having said all this, what kind of curriculum should a GPP offer? Inevitably, there will be diversity around a core given differences in scholarly talent, academic histories, university funding, socio-cultural systems, levels of economic development, political circumstances, and even conceptions of national interest. Academic institutions and choices are conditioned by broader academic, financial, social, economic, political, and geopolitical settings, and it would be unwise and unrealistic to suppose that they can exist in a vacuum, altogether free to do as they please.

Arguably, a specifically global version of the policy studies would include the following elements:

1. *Training in constituent disciplines*, some of which may need to be more broadly construed than they have been in "traditional" approaches to policy education. These will certainly include economics, politics and management (as before). But a strong argument can be made — and may be worth exploring in this conference — that a far greater focus than in the past on the global commons and the interface of the public and private sectors is warranted in the GPP curriculum. It is a remarkable fact that the traditional public policy and administration core curriculum has no particular place for international relations or affairs; there is no body of knowledge about the governance of the global commons, for instance, that one can expect any graduate of a school of public policy to reasonably possess, unlike (for instance) the

assumption that all would have been exposed to the theory of the firm in their basic microeconomics course.

Likewise, it is hard to argue that the core curricula of the vast majority of policy schools adequately prepare graduates for the heavy degree of participation — and even dominance in some sectors and countries — of private sector actors in determining the destiny of the "commons", whether at local, national or global levels. A recent review by Jeffrey Straussman of the core public administration courses taught in MPA programmes in the US concluded that a "visitor from another planet" reading these course syllabi would conclude that the private sector has almost nothing to do with the way public governance plays out. If that ever *was* true, it certainly no longer is the case; and GPPs wishing to stay true to 21st Century realities will, moving forward, need to take stock of this through curriculum innovation.

2. *A focus on integrative problem-solving.* This arguably is and always has been the hallmark of professional policy education at its best. Students are not taught a smattering of economics, politics, management and other disciplines so as to be second-rate economists and political scientists. Rather, they learn frameworks and skills in these disciplines so that they will be first-rate creative problem-solvers for challenges that clearly have multiple, interdependent dimensions and implications; or to use terms popular in leadership studies, so that they can solve *adaptive* rather than merely *technical* problems confronting their societies. The challenge, as always, will be to develop pedagogical methods that facilitate this integrative approach, and to develop the incentives and academic culture that supports faculty *modelling* this behaviour rather than teaching comfortably within their subject-matter silos.

3. *Functional and geographical specializations and an appreciation of the importance of context.* The GPP curriculum will undoubtedly need to go beyond disciplinary courses to include offerings that can add up to a functional and/or geographical specialization; the ability to combine, for instance, social policy expertise with an substantive appreciation of the contemporary South Asian or Latin American political and economic context and trends. Indeed, what may ultimately mark the graduate of a GPP is the ability to think

subtly and productively about the importance of *context* on policy design and implementation.

Context and Curriculum: An Asian Thought Experiment

To extend this thought experiment, how might an emphasis on the importance of context play out in Asia, for instance, in ways that might challenge the boundaries of the "traditional" policy curriculum? What is the broader context in which public policy programmes will operate in Asia? Consider the following.

First of all, socially, Asian societies are usually highly plural in terms of ethnic, religious, and linguistic affiliations. The relationship of individuals to communities is still strong. Kinship matters considerably (though, admittedly, with variation). How to manage this diversity in the interest of social peace and progress is a constant concern in much of Asia.

Secondly, economically, Asia offers a heterogeneous landscape with several countries in East Asia and Southeast Asia that have advanced up to and in some cases beyond Western levels and others that are in the mid-range while yet others are at low levels of per capita income and industrialization. Still, the overwhelming number of states is in the mid or low range. Sustained economic growth over the next three to four decades and eliminating poverty constitute central challenges. Transitioning from a rural-agricultural economy to an urban-manufacturing-cum-service economy lies ahead. These are societies that are struggling to achieve higher levels of human development, build modern infrastructure and communication systems, and achieve a balance between economic development and environmental sustainability. The mid and low range economies also feature income and wealth disparities. Demographically, they continue to grow, even as rates of growth have slowed. The demographic profile features a very large number of young people in search of education and jobs. How to manage both kinds of economic systems but particularly the mid and low range systems and how to take them to higher levels of economic development while ensuring social justice and environmental stability is a huge challenge, one that is complicated by issues relating to fiscal health, the state of the global economy and of a country's external sector, and state regulation and simultaneously de-regulation of the economy.

Thirdly, politically, Asia features governments that have intervened in all sectors of social and economic life as part of nation building. Asian governments have a mixed record in delivering clean and efficient administration, providing basic services, ensuring law and order, and responding to popular demands and participation. How to build institutions that carry out the will of the political leadership in these and other areas and yet empower and respect the rights of citizens is a crucial pivot of Asian politics. This basic problem of governance continues to challenge Asia.

Fourth, geopolitically, Asia features a number of conflicts which divide it and which could explode into violence. These rivalries and conflicts pivot about border and other territorial quarrels, relative power and status, and national identity and pride. Asia has a history of war — interstate as well as internal. Its explosive economic growth could be a force for integration but could also fuel geopolitical rivalries which outpace the ability of its normative and institutional structures to deal with conflict. Asian security is complicated by the presence of four nuclear powers (China, India, Pakistan, and North Korea), some of the world's largest militaries, terrorism and insurgency with links that are transnational (both regional and global), and the mounting problems of the global commons which are potentially "game changers". How to manage Asia's geopolitics and sub-conventional violence is a key policy challenge.

This context suggests that a curriculum for GPP in Asia might include offerings — some core and some elective — in the following four fields:

- Managing ethnically, religiously, and linguistically plural societies
- A sustainable transition from a predominantly rural/agricultural, regulated, and autarkic economy to an urban/manufacturing-service, marketising, and internationalising economy in a globalising world
- Institution building in political systems that must balance government leadership and responsiveness
- Peace and security in Asia and the problems of the global commons

In Asia, if the above context has been properly depicted, a GPP curriculum will have to debate a number of issues.

What core courses should it offer? What kinds of specializations are students and clients looking for and what kind of electives therefore need to be made available?

What is the appropriate balance between core courses and electives? How multi-disciplinary and global should a public policy programme aim to be in terms of curriculum, research, students, and faculty? What kind of pedagogy works best for various programmes of study — for fresh post-graduates looking for careers in the civil service, business, or NGO sectors; for junior and mid-career serving civil servants; and for professionals in other fields who take time out from, or are looking to change, their chosen career paths? What is the balance between teaching, fundamental research, and policy consultancy for the faculty?

What kind of curriculum a GPP programme offers is in the end also dependent on the academic talent that is available, the academic history of a country as well as of the public policy school concerned, and funding. Clearly, some part of curriculum offerings arises from the academic talent in the faculty. New faculty hiring can help change curricular direction, but resistance from older faculty can stand in the way of the infusion of new talent and a reordering of core and elective courses. Academic history counts for something as well. A programme that has taken a particular direction, and has had success in it, will find it difficult to change in response to changing contexts and demands. Path dependency and the fact of success can bring about lock-ins. Funding too is crucial. The curricular coat must be cut according to the financial cloth.

We suggest therefore that the future of global public policy is plural. The view that global public policy education and research will or should be convergent contains a kernel of truth — there are some obvious commonalities across public policy schools; but equally there are differences, and these could well increase rather than decrease in the foreseeable future given academic, funding, economic, socio-cultural, political, and geopolitical differences.

What Can GPPN Do?

By way of conclusion, we offer some brief thoughts on the role of the GPPN.

GPPN is not, as some might fear, on the way to becoming an accreditation institution. To be a global public policy school will not require an institution to submit to criteria laid down by a GPPN. The world of public policy programmes is far too plural for any such effort at norm enforcement. GPPN is not a full-blooded association with rules and regulations.

The GPPN, as we see it, is a talk shop in large measure. It is a forum for the discussion of best practices in an evolving field, a field in flux and a field in the midst of self-reflection. It is an opportunity therefore for participants to refine their thinking, through debate, with others around the world.

GPPN cannot and should not aim to bring about a uniformity of curriculum and research priorities. Uniformity is scarcely possible given different histories, contexts, and capabilities. Nor is it desirable, for as long as we can see into the future. Pluralism is almost always a good thing, and monocultures are almost always a bad thing. Monocultures are prone to being wiped out by disease strains they cannot combat. Academic monocultures could lead to academic extinction. The world may change in unexpected ways; in fact, this is likely. Pluralism in academic life is vital in confronting a rapidly changing world. What seems irrelevant in public policy programmes today may be extremely relevant in the future.

In any case, diversity in global public policy programmes has produced one of the more material achievements of GPPN, namely, student and (less so) faculty collaboration and exchange. If all GPP programmes were more or less the same, there would be little or no need for students and faculty from different countries and programmes to interact.

Finally, GPPN is an invitation to others to join in the conversation about the future of public policy programmes. Public policy programmes are proliferating quite rapidly including in Africa, Asia, and Latin America. This is an existential reality. Whether or not public policy as a field merits a separate programme or not is being largely settled by the start of so many new programmes rather than by a deep and decisive debate in the original home of these programmes, namely, the US. These new programmes will also have an impact on curriculum. They will adopt some of the norms of the original programmes, but they will also invent their own pathways. As global public policy studies go global, we should be in for exciting times.

Appendix B

A Sampling of Research Projects and Milestones[1]

A few themes and milestones of the LKY School's research in the first eight years are described below:

- Asian countries have experienced rapid economic growth and social development in recent years, and the region presents many opportunities for comparative health policy research, including studying innovative practices in the delivery, financing and regulation of health systems. The past Asian and current global fiscal crises, coupled with the emergence of new infectious diseases and the prospects of regional pandemics, have thrown the vulnerabilities of many healthcare systems into sharp relief. What are the regional lessons and what would be the health impact of economic crises? With future prospects of trade further opening up, healthcare markets in both private and public sectors in Asia will be subjected to more competition arising from medical tourism and growth of the biomedical industry. It is timely to take stock and monitor the trends and issues in healthcare systems in the region and identify from a comparative perspective, the challenges that have arisen with changing social, economic and political conditions, and the ways in which governments are responding to these challenges. The changing roles and interface among the public, private and voluntary sectors; the extent of public-private participation in healthcare towards balancing the objectives

---

1   This section draws from material provided by LKY School professors and research fellows. See also *Compendium of Research 2009–2010*, Singapore, Lee Kuan Yew School of Public Policy, National University of Singapore, 2011.

of socio-economic development; and their implications in terms of differential access, quality and affordability for the public are all themes that need to be better understood. These areas are at the core of research by a few LKY School faculty and fellows, led by Phua Kai Hong. Publications on these topics have included a special series of the *Lancet* journal on health in Southeast Asia; regular *Asian Trends Monitoring* reports (with support from The Rockefeller Foundation), articles, book chapters, op-eds and case studies.

- M. Ramesh, Wu Xun, Scott Fritzen, Eduardo Araral and others continue to advance comparative public policy research with their work on public management, public services, anti-corruption, global governance, pension reform, foreign aid and the role of multilateral institutions, public-private partnerships and other themes. Their recent collaboration has produced several books, including *Transforming Asian Governance* (Routledge, 2009); *Reasserting the Public in Public Services* (Routledge, 2009); and *The Public Policy Primer: Managing the Public Policy Process* (Routledge, 2010).

- M. Ramesh and Wu Xun have collaborated on publications in *Social Science and Medicine* and *Development and Change*. Their work highlights the pitfalls of healthcare reforms currently being pursued in Asia, especially in China. They argue that expansion of health insurance and increase in expenditure without reform of provision and provider payment systems is misguided and likely to fail.

- Ora-orn Poocharoen's research has elucidated the role that bureaucratic structures and rules have played in the still-unfolding deadly conflict in southern Thailand. These structures and rules have shaped bureaucratic behaviour and citizens' mistrust. An increasing number of citizens are taking up public sector positions, creating pressure for institutions to change. Poocharoen recommends that, going forward, the Thai government must start an open discussion for autonomy in the South. Poocharoen is also conducting research on performance management in the public sector and collaborative governance and anti-corruption.

- In their project on "New Approaches to Building Markets in Asia", Toby Carroll and Darryl Jarvis examine ongoing efforts by state, private and non-governmental entities to build the regulatory and other institutional elements now deemed essential for markets and development. The research project, which involves roughly 75 people from around the world, has three core components that each focuses upon a particular set of institutions/stakeholders involved in and/or impacted by market-building measures in Asia: public organisations, private organisations and citizens. A paper by Carroll examines the role of the International Finance Corporation (IFC) and its promotion of new pro-private sector modalities that are overhauling development practice in Southeast Asia. Another by Jarvis looks at the political economy of building regulatory states in the Global South, presenting the Indonesian electricity sector as a case that suggests we should take another look at many of the assumptions that underpin current reform agendas.

- Too little scholarship in public policy considers how multiple kinds of concurrently applied policies interact with one another when applied for similar outcomes. In their article published in the top-ranked *Journal of Policy Analysis and Management*, Boyd Fuller and Vu Minh Khuong use a simple, computer simulation to open up this black box and develop seven testable hypotheses for future, rigorous testing into the interaction among multiple policy approaches. The authors look at three policy approaches that, respectively, exhort, provide incentives for, and increase the competency of private sector participants to collaborate as they seek to improve their businesses, work together to improve communities and so on. This article won the Academy of Management's Best Article Award, Public and Non-Profit Division, in 2011.

- Apart from directly writing about political institutions, principles and practices in Singapore, Kenneth Paul Tan has also made out-of-the-box attempts to interpret Singapore's political culture, public administration and policymaking. He undertakes unconventional analysis of Singaporean culture (including art and popular cultural forms such as cinema), making innovative use of theory (for instance, contemporary feminist psychoanalytical theory) and literary tropes (drawing, for instance, on classical mythology). Among Tan's recent publications are "The Transformation of Meritocracy" in *Management of Success: Singapore Revisited* and "*Pontianaks*, Ghosts, and the Possessed:

Female Monstrosity and National Anxiety in Singapore Cinema" in the *Asian Studies Review*.

- In research funded by the MacArthur Foundation, Benjamin Sovacool and fellow colleagues investigated the interaction between energy governance and energy security in Asia. The project produced case studies focusing on the emerging architecture of energy development assistance programmes, with a special emphasis on renewable energy. Cases covered include Laos, Mongolia, Malaysia, Papua New Guinea, China, Nepal, Bangladesh, Sri Lanka and Indonesia.

- Eduardo Araral's research on "The Strategic Games that Donors and Bureaucrats" play has reignited a debate among water governance scholars on how to reform the equilibrium of perverse incentives between donors and bureaucrats. Araral, along with another LKY School faculty member, Vu Minh Khuong, has been commissioned by the Drafting Committee of Vietnam's 2011–2020 Socio-Economic Development Plan to provide recommendations for strategic governance reforms.

- Asit Biswas has written and edited numerous books and articles on water policy and governance. One of his more recent publications is an edited volume (with Cecilia Tortajada and Dogan Altinbilek) entitled *Impacts of Large Dams: A Global Assessment.* The book presents in-depth case studies to address the debate between those who argue that large dams are essential to meet the world's increasing water demands, and that the benefits outweigh the costs; and those who argue that the social and environmental costs of large dams far outweigh the benefits. Biswas and Cecilia Tortajada are also completing a book on "The Singapore Water Story".

- Huang Jing and Kanti Bajpai, working under the aegis of the Centre on Asia and Globalisation, are conducting research on China-India conflict management and cooperation. Other faculty members and fellows are also doing work on China and India's economics, politics and foreign relations. In a few years, the School hopes to generate a body of work that will consolidate knowledge and understanding of key dynamics and actors in two of the world's most important countries today.

- Chen Kang, a senior economist at the School, studies China's macroeconomic policy, the economic role of government and China's regional economies, and how these are integrated and interact with the centre. Using econometric modelling, Chen's work emphasises the institutional features of regional economies and their complicated responses to policy changes. Recent publications include a co-authored Asian edition of *Principles of Economics*, and articles and papers on China's macroeconomic situation, the impact of intergovernmental transfers in China, cultural differences between Tibetans and Han Chinese in ultimatum bargaining experiments, and others.
- Astrid S. Tuminez published "Rising to the Top? A Report on Women's Leadership in Asia" in April 2012. In collaboration with the Asia Society, the report was launched at the 2012 Women Leaders of New Asia Summit held in April in Shanghai and Zhenjiang in China. Numerous newspaper, radio and television outlets around the world covered the report, which the United Nations Development Program (UNDP) is also translating into Vietnamese and disseminating in Vietnam. The Association of Pacific Rim Universities (APRU) has also distributed the report to university presidents and other senior executives. Faculty members Ora-orn Poocharoen, Suzaina Kadir, Kenneth Paul Tan and Jonathan Marshall also collaborated with Tuminez and other colleagues from the NUS Faculty of Arts and Sciences on a workshop on women's pathways to leadership in Asia.